Praise

'A brilliant read that mentors, inspires and keeps you hooked. A perfect book for aspiring or experienced entrepreneurs and leaders.'
   — **Lloyd Glanville PhD, The University of Hull**

'The road to "true" fulfilment is littered with potholes and speed cameras. This book equips the reader with a vehicle that softens the bumps and sees the cameras before it's too late, allowing the driver to "truly" enjoy the ride.'
   — **Dr Simon Whitaker**

'Working 60hrs plus, a slave to the machine? Then please take a copy of *Eight Figure Entrepreneur*. This book will take you on a journey of self-realisation, it will challenge your mindset and purpose. The vision, presentation, content and motivation shown within this book will inspire you to apply the knowledge, information and techniques it contains into your own life, both personally and professionally. I started reading it and couldn't put it down.'
   — **Glenn Paddison, Director, MKM**

'This book is both thought-provoking and instructive. It provides you with high-level concept thinking, while concurrently imparting practical, detailed methods to develop and grow your

company from a one-man-band to a high-achieving team that meet your business and personal aims.'
— **Sarah McDermott, Managing Director, Maison Parfaite**

'A fast-track guide to business mastery – this insightful and intelligent read provides step-by-step instructions on how to excel in leadership and find fulfilment and success along the way. Once you've digested the contents of this captivating book, failure will no longer be an option!'
— **Bruce Daniels, Director, Bruda**

'A thoughtful and insightful study of the experiences of an undoubtedly entrepreneurial individual in setting up and running successful businesses – that are now among the leaders, if not the real leader in their fields. It manages not to be an ego trip – indeed it includes several caveats about the dangers of being too self-assured and becoming too business-centred, while also providing much useful guidance. For owners/directors who are sufficiently open-minded to realise that there is always something new that you can learn from others, this will be good reading.'
— **Martyn Benson, Principal, Bradmarsh Templar**

8
FIGURE
ENTREPRENEUR

SCALE UP WHILE LIVING A BALANCED, ADVENTUROUS AND HAPPY LIFE

PAUL LUEN

R∃THINK PRESS

First published in Great Britain in 2020
by Rethink Press (www.rethinkpress.com)

Contents

Introduction   1

1   The Success Trap   9

Measuring success   13

Flip it   15

Reflect and 'zoom out'   16

Checklist: Self-diagnosis   19

2   Rebalancing   21

Reset   22

Reinvest   24

Prioritise outcomes for others   26

Surrender your ego and practise humility   27

Work on your business, not in it   30

Checklist: Rebalancing   33

3   Discovering Purpose And Values   35

The eulogy   35

Starting out 37

Discover your purpose 38

Discover your values 40

Business purpose and values 42

Strategy follows purpose 46

Checklist: Discover your purpose and values 48

4 Winning The Talent War 51

How attractive is your business? 52

Company show reel 53

Advertising the job 54

Where to find candidates 58

Filtering the applicants 60

Virtual talent 66

Checklist: Winning the talent war 67

5 Develop And Retain Superstars 69

Pre-boarding 69

On-boarding 71

Probation 72

Cost of bad hires 74

Responsibility and freedom 75

Continuous professional development 77

Long-term incentive plan 81

Abhorrent annual appraisals! 81

Engagement surveys 82

Sickness 85

Exit interviews 87

Checklist: Develop and retain superstars 88

6 Innovation And Intellectual Property 89

Filtering your light bulb moments 91

Vanilla versus rum and raisin 93

Positioning 95

Premium offerings with strong margins
and recurring revenue 97

Fail fast! 99

Portfolio of assets 101

Protecting your assets 102

Checklist: innovation and
intellectual property 103

7 Marketing 105

Specialist talent 108

Content 110

Audience 114

Website 116

Automation 117

KPIs 119

Checklist: Marketing 120

8 Sales 121

Sales method 122

Selecting your team 123

Sales incentives 125

Sales planning and reporting 127

Developing sales skills 128

Qualifying 131

Sales tools 135

Major bids 136

Negotiation 139

Sales channels 142

KPIs 144

Checklist: Sales 145

9 Systems And Processes 147

Software systems and automation 150

Rhythms and rituals 151

Leadership meeting rhythms 153

Parkinson's law 157

The 'parking lot' 157

Avoiding interruptions and distractions 158

Checklist: systems and processes 160

10 Inspiring Leadership 161

The CEO 163

General leadership environment 165

Transparency 166

Situational leadership 168

Succession planning 169

360-degree surveys 171

My key leadership attributes 172

Checklist: Inspiring leadership 173

11 It's Your Turn Now 175

Be and experience who you are 179

My truths 181

Breaking free 182

Checklist: It's your turn now 183

Conclusion 185

Acknowledgements 189

The Author 191

Introduction

I've made a lot of mistakes in life, too many to count. Some were absolute whoppers. Since I started my first business in the late 1990s, I've played hero and villain in many weird and wonderful stories along the way. Looking back, it's hard to believe some of the things I've done. As I recently turned the big five-oh, I began to reflect on the journey that's taken me through boom and almost bust, massive highs with horrible lows, and episodes of abject frustration contrasted with periods of peace and fulfilment. I wouldn't change a thing.

As I write this, I've recently sold my second business start-up for an eight-figure sum. Seeing big numbers on a bank statement as the transaction completed was an anti-climax though. I thought that the culmination of years of blood, sweat and tears would feel so different. I celebrated with a bottle of fizz at home and ordered an Indian takeaway with my wife and kids. Rock star!

In truth, for too long success was all about the money for me. Now, I've learned that living a balanced life and being fit and healthy, while still remaining meaningfully connected to friends and family, is what it's really all about. Plain and simple.

My epiphany came in one of my favourite places in the world, Ibiza. My friend Rico inadvertently smashed me with a huge cannonball that I didn't see coming and I'm eternally grateful for what he said to me. In the midst of the carnage of a boys' weekend on the 'White Isle', he'd noticed I was a shadow of myself. 'You've got mojo-nitis,' he joked, and that was the start of a journey culminating in this book.

I have survived, navigated my way through the hard knocks and, what's more, I've been lucky enough to prosper when others have been less fortunate. I say 'lucky' because I've made some deliberate and tough choices – the kind that are much easier *not* to make.

As I've shifted my youthful thinking from that of a selfish, driven pr!ck to that of serving others and helping them achieve their goals, my own success has accelerated and amplified – opportunities keep revealing themselves far and wide. It got me thinking that there might be a story to tell from this working-class lad from Hull who started with 'nowt', worked his ass off, did some good stuff and was keen to help others do the same. I want to share my mistakes, experiences and learnings with anyone who can empathise with the struggles of life, family and careers. When everyone on social media seems to be living like rock stars, the pressure to do the same has never been greater. The reality is much different – as you'll probably know if you're searching for greater success and happiness.

It doesn't matter whether you're a corporate manager, a solopreneur, an entrepreneur, an employee in a small business, an intrapreneur or just starting out on your journey – I'm certain some or all of the challenges I've encountered will resonate with you. You're not alone. My aim is to help you avoid many of the mistakes I've made, and the pain that I've been through. I want to play a part in accelerating the success you dream of, so you'll be happier, healthier and live longer as a result. My hope then is that you'll 'pay it forward' to help others.

I'm fortunate now to coach and mentor a wide range of people at different stages of their journey. What I see so often at the start is a lack of focus and awareness around the importance of their professional and personal development. The greatest investment anyone can make is in their own development, as you can never earn beyond what you learn. Continuing professional development is the big differentiator in the cutthroat and highly competitive world of business: do it or die! In the information age, the people who can get the fastest access to the latest teachings, absorb that info and then gainfully apply it at a breakneck speed are the ones who'll rise to the top.

What you'll read in this book isn't rocket science, but there are some fundamental guiding principles that have worked for me and the teams I've led across multiple businesses and sectors. Through an obsessive focus on personal development, I've discovered the tools and mindset to dig myself out of holes, navigate challenging times and get the most from opportunities when they reveal themselves. Together they create a real sense of purpose, a huge sense of personal fulfilment, increased energy and a great workplace culture that attracts the best people: those who passionately serve each other, the business and, ultimately, the customers. That all begins with discovering who you really are and what your business stands for.

In Chapters One to Three I'll begin our journey of discovery together by inviting you to take a long, close look at where you are with your life now – not just in a business context, but in all areas of your life. There's no judgement attached to this; it's simply a diagnostic check-in with yourself about what's going on with you at this moment. All I ask is that you reflect on this as honestly as you can. You might not feel 100%

comfortable with the answers, but that doesn't mean that what you're doing is wrong, or bad, in any way. The intent is to give *you* the space and time to connect with the hopes, dreams and aspirations that *you* started out with. Are you living up to your expectations? That might mean you need to spend some time identifying, or articulating, your real sense of purpose – the thing that gets you out of bed in the morning with renewed energy every day. If, like many over-stressed executives, you can't sleep well at night, perhaps there's a mismatch between your pursuit of purpose and pleasure. If so, reading this book is a good way to discover the tools and techniques that will help you find that better balance.

In Chapters Four and Five I'll describe the techniques I've learned that take away much of the pain of recruiting and retaining the best of the talent available so that, crucially, they're aligned to your values from day one. Recruitment is an area of major concern for the executives I coach, many of whom find that they spend too much time going around in circles trying to find people who, in a competitive jobs market, will hop from job to job. The critical component of all business success is the quality of your people, who need to be working in a great culture with rhythm to truly flourish. By adopting a nurturing mindset and a cohesive set of processes and systems that are designed to bring out the best in everyone, success will follow.

As we move into Chapter Six, I'll describe what I've done across my businesses to create an innovation culture where everyone shares collective responsibility for bringing new ideas to the fore. I'll show you a process that works to generate and filter ideas. It's then about refining them into a portfolio of assets that are highly differentiated so they stand out and deliver compelling financial returns, being mindful to surrender your ego and fail fast when you spot the signs.

Chapters Seven and Eight reveal some of the guiding principles of marketing and sales that determine the ability of any organisation to get the best returns on their assets. I'll share my simple A^2 principle, which will guide your decisions so that you reach the widest possible audience. I'll also share my approach to dominating content marketing in specific niches and, once you've attracted prospects, how to take them through a consistent sales process to maximise your win rate and shorten the sales cycle.

Applying a 'systems thinking' approach is the focus of Chapter Nine, and I'll share in detail the rituals and rhythms that underpin the successful execution of any business strategy and maintain a healthy organisation. You'll also gain insights into how to get more done in less time and what the distraction of constant interruptions is likely costing you.

In Chapters Ten and Eleven you will begin to see how your business and your life will be transformed when you use the tools and techniques in this book to marry purpose and pleasure so you can ascend to a new form of leadership. I want this book to be a wake-up call for highly driven people who have something missing, like I did. Unless somebody shows us a different way, we'll end up with a society of stressed, unfit and unhappy people who are going to live shorter, less fulfilled lives. Until you recalibrate who you are and why you're here, nothing will change: the great success you've dreamed of will probably always elude you, if not in the short term then in the long term. More will never be enough.

Thankfully, I've done the hard work and I've learned from my mistakes. I count myself lucky that I had my own wake-up call and ran the hard yards to educate myself. I needed to find a different way to run my life and my businesses, and I needed to learn how to implement some new principles of business in a different way. My big realisation was that when we surrender ego, put ourselves at the bottom of an organisation's hierarchy and become more curious, we create moments when we can nurture others to succeed. My bigger realisation was that in helping others to succeed, we also succeed ourselves. That feels good, better than any material gains. That clarity on what gives us real pleasure nourishes a deeply felt sense of purpose in our professional lives, which allows us to enjoy our life to the max.

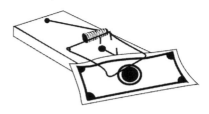

1
The Success Trap

When I started my first company, success to me was all about how quickly the business was growing, how much money I was earning or which expensive car I could buy next. It took me a long time to realise that more was never enough. I always wanted more, but when I got it, it meant little. As I turned forty, got married and my first child was on the way, I had an epiphany. I began to recognise that there was more to life than simply defining myself by career 'success'. I'd been a totally selfish pr!ck up to this point – sorry, everyone!

Luckily, my epiphany warned me (just in time to prevent total burnout) that I needed to slow down to be able to speed up. Counterintuitive as that might sound when a career or business is the priority, this gradual recalibration of my life enabled me to grow in more ways than I could have expected. I grew not only as a person, but also as an entrepreneur and leader – to the point that at the beginning of 2019, I sold one of my businesses to a major public limited company for an eight-figure sum. This amazing result would have been impossible without my epiphany.

Creating your own version of super-success is never easy. Reaching the top requires a huge amount of effort and dedication. You have to put in a dispro-portionate amount of hard work, expend bucketloads of personal energy in the process, and come back for more every day with unwavering resilience. If success was easy, everybody would be achieving it. But not everybody can, and it takes a special type of person. I'm hoping that's you.

No matter what business or career you're in, I suspect we have a lot in common. Nothing compares to dream-ing up that brilliant, fantastic idea; from the first flush of excitement as it takes shape in the mind's eye, to creating the commercial vehicle to realise the dream. Then you start translating your idea into action and chasing down leads to secure the 'deal of the century'. I can easily identify with that portrait from my early days as an entrepreneur, when I saw my first inde-pendent business idea grow into a global enterprise. All the while, I was obsessed with the business. I was barely able to keep up with myself as my endorphins kicked into overdrive, the adrenaline flowed freely through my veins and my mind raced as I tweaked and refined my proposition. The pursuit of business perfection and growth is intoxicating, and it carries us as we relentlessly chase success. We target, we home in, we 'go in for the kill' and by the end of that process, we may gain the trophies or bear the scars to show for it, over and over again. Losing, giving up or failing are simply not options. Does any of that resonate with you – 'no pain, no gain', right?

Since I turned forty, I've been convinced that the pain *can* far outweigh the *marginal* gain, and if you're reading this book then you might be feeling the same way. No matter how much you've achieved and 'enjoyed' the trappings of your 'success', somewhere deep inside there's an intuitive awareness of another narrative that's telling a different story.

If you're like me, you probably try to bury that awareness as much as you can, because that's easier to do. For me, it used to be 'business, business, business'. As a consequence, my family, friends, children and health often took second place. Realising how unfulfilling it had become, I began to take more notice of that little voice nagging away in the back of my head. Like it or not, your hidden voice is questioning the sacrifices you've made on your journey to where you are now. When you really begin to inspect your immediate surroundings, it feels more like an empty destination. Success might have carried you there on an all-expenses-paid, first-class flight, but what's the point if you've actually arrived on your own, having gradually lost touch with your family, your friends – and, more importantly –yourself? It's a conundrum, especially if your dream has rewarded you well. Despite everything you've achieved, do you sometimes feel like your life lacks meaning, balance and general fulfilment?

Back when you started out, you might have been committed and driven. Your ambition and hunger for success gave you energy and provided so much pleasure in the purpose. These days, in the moments you allow for some introspection, you may find yourself admitting that the gloss that once shone for all the world to see has faded. What was once a rollercoaster ride feels more like a treadmill as your business or career plateaus and stagnates, and you're no longer certain where you're heading to, or even why. Is this the end result you've worked so hard for? Have you come as far as you can go, or are you missing out on something you don't yet have the courage to identify? Not only is this inner conflict affecting you personally, but it's also preventing your growth. Perhaps that's why now is the time to take a good look at yourself, your ritualised life and the people around you, and reflect on what you need to do to get to that next level. If so, I understand how you feel.

Measuring success

In my experience, many entrepreneurs and highly driven people measure their success in metrics and not in terms of how happy they are. By metrics, I mean the size of their salary or their material gains. I did this myself. In reality, when I bought that first Lamborghini it didn't actually make me feel any happier once I'd driven it for the first time and tried (unsuccessfully) to park it in my garage. Did I feel any more successful or fulfilled? No!

For me, the metrics – the 'stuff' I bought or things I did – were a way of keeping score of the success of my business. It never occurred to me to ask myself what it all meant. Was it contributing to my happiness, my health, my relationships, my balance, my fitness or my overall wellbeing? The simple answer is that it wasn't. I was only sacrificing my ultimate wellbeing for material gain.

Social media and the proliferation of other people's 'good news' stories make a big contribution to the pressure that people feel under to keep up with others. I encounter numerous executives who feel that they're not achieving their best when they see the glossy, successful stories that their contemporaries post online. That's not reality; it's a curated version of it. Posts on social media rarely, if ever, portray the struggles that people just like us are dealing with every day. Instead we're fed the message that life's great for everybody, and everybody else is being successful. The perception this leaves us with is that if our life isn't that great in comparison then we must be failing, so we need to work harder, spend more time away from home, and do, do, do more. It becomes the 'rat race' – unhealthy, unsustainable and destructive.

The most important point here is that everyone can't be exceptional or the best, because then *no one* is exceptional. If we are geared only towards being exceptional, many of us will leave this world feeling a great sense of disappointment. Achieving success is possible, but that success is relative, and it shouldn't be at the expense of losing sight of who we are and why we do what we do. It's about keeping a 360-degree perspective so we can see the whole picture surrounding us.

Speeding towards huge profits may work for some in the short term, but without the back-up fuel in our tanks, your engine will cut out and you will stall. You don't need to be the hardest-working, most stressed person in your organisation – au contraire! To speed up, you need to slow down and be one of the *least* stressed people. If you allow yourself plenty of headspace to think about and work on the business, you'll then be able to work on growing those around you.

Having been on this journey myself, adjusting my speed immediately released me from the pressure of needing to be at the front of the race. I stopped paying attention to my competitors and peers or measuring myself against their publicly declared successes (real or embellished). Instead, I found the space to breathe. In that space I gradually discovered there was room for me to think about how I could diversify and amplify my business goals and grow my businesses' success even more than I'd dared to believe. In that space, I rediscovered my joie de vivre.

Flip it

As my career evolved I saw it was time to start letting go; I realised that the reason the business had plateaued was because I had put myself at its epicentre and I was suffocating the business and damaging myself in the process, missing out on time with my wife, children and friends. Some of my achievements also felt hollow, because they were selfish.

I realised that this was the right time to empower people with more responsibility and freedom. By letting go of some of the 'small stuff', I was able to focus on some of the bigger stuff that wasn't getting done – and this is where the real magic happens.

A key principle to grasp is that *nobody works for you*. Everyone works for themselves. Your job is to get curious about the innermost wants and needs of the team you work in or lead, then focus on serving and supporting them so they can fulfil themselves. Offer yourself the chance to pause and see where you can step back and hand over trust and responsibility to those who work with you. By setting that example, you can support others to lead and free yourself from the minutiae of business that can easily be managed by your teams. That creates space for you to work on new ideas that will take your business from stagnation to innovation. By doing this, you will achieve success faster and leverage more areas of the business than before. Your stress levels will plummet, thanks to the more controlled pace that you're operating at. Instead of being in a vicious circle, you'll be in a virtuous one.

Again, I would encourage you to think and act almost counterintuitively and lead your business from the bottom up, in a supportive style that is balanced with an appropriate level of challenge. Even the tallest sky-scrapers are supported by their deep foundations. Only when I stopped leading from the top did I realise that I could work across multiple enterprises at the same time and be strong and enduring as a result.

Reflect and 'zoom out'

Hard times deliver hard lessons, and when one of my businesses faced potential disaster after the global financial crisis of 2008, I learned that neither I nor the business was bulletproof. Facing the fear of failure was a moment of real pain. Pain comes in all forms, and if your enterprise or career is beginning to give you more pain than pleasure, this is your opportunity to diagnose the root cause before it becomes unbearable and debilitating.

Being an entrepreneur or pursuing a successful career has to mean more than putting in at least sixty hours a week, every week. Of course, any new venture or significant step up the career ladder requires hard work and takes time, but if you lose that connection with the first flush of excitement, the adrenaline rush can fade. Reaching such a moment of stagnation, crisis or consciousness is a catalyst for you to reignite that early sense of curiosity, wonderment and hope for your dreams – but this time, you can bring with you all those fantastic qualities and experiences you've gathered along the way. Whatever your chosen destination, once you have diagnosed the pain that is impeding your progress towards it, you can find the treatment that works best for you and your business, whether that's creating an exit strategy or striving to be a better version of yourself. Allowing yourself the time to have this conversation about 'success' is the first step to removing the barriers in achieving your full potential as the leader you aim to be.

I want you to go back even further in your thoughts to the time when you initially dreamed up your business concept or started that new job. Think back to how high your energy levels were then compared with recently. How much has that energy reserve been depleted? You might not have been looking after yourself, stoking your engine with the wrong type of fuel, which is beginning to affect your performance. If so, don't beat yourself up about it: it's the default position we can find ourselves in. Now is the perfect opportunity to refuel, reconnect with your source of inspiration and let that inspiration flow freely again.

This isn't anything to be scared of. At times, I've deliberately suppressed how I felt because it was easier than admitting to myself that I didn't feel energised or fulfilled. I was also worried that reflecting was a self-indulgent, unprofitable exercise, but I now realise that this may have been a result of social and cultural conditioning. Not long ago, men, in particular, would never admit that they had a softer, more vulnerable edge, and they certainly wouldn't talk about it. Articulating anything of the sort was tantamount to weakness or worse. Suicide is still one of the biggest causes of early mortality among males in the UK and, according to statistics published by the Samaritans, men are three times as likely to take their own lives as women are, with the highest suicide rate among men aged forty-five to forty-nine.[1] Men are prone to suppressing their feelings and don't allow themselves to observe them. When they do, it provides a real sense of freedom, because that's a gateway to connecting with purpose.

---

1   'Suicide facts and figures', www.samaritans.org/about-samaritans/research-policy/suicide-facts-and-figures

I've discovered that the more I open up and the more I'm honest about just being a normal guy, irrespective of how I earn my living, the deeper I can connect with the people I care most about and work with, and this fosters a greater mutual understanding. It allows me to live my business life authentically, without being disrupted by any negative criticism. I'm positively comfortable about letting go, and these days I'm completely unconcerned about what other people might think of me. That represents a real sense of freedom to focus on how I want to live my life. When I compare this with the 'old days', when I was acting as the head honcho in a top-down, 'command and control' way, I can see there was no freedom in that at all.

Checklist: Self-diagnosis

- Are you continually striving for more?

- When will more ever be enough? Does it feel hollow?

- What are you neglecting or sacrificing due to work commitments?

- Do you often compare your life's successes negatively with other people's?

- How often do you feel like you're trapped on a treadmill?

- Do you feel a need to work harder than most and be at the centre of everything?

- How often do you feel wired but tired, working at least sixty hours a week but still it's not enough?

- Can you easily concentrate on deep intellectual tasks rather than taking solace in sending emails, browsing social media or playful surfing?

- How easy do you find it to relax rather than always being anxious to do something?

- How often do you get irritated by simple things?

- How's your drinking, your nutrition and your general health?

- How's your libido?

- How easy is it for you to fall or stay asleep?

- Are you in a permanent state of rush and arousal?

- What of life's pleasures are you missing out on by relentlessly pursuing materialistic goals?

- How 'present' are you generally with your family and friends, and how likely are you to succumb to distractions or interruptions from messages?

- Which friends have you lost touch with that you used to really value and enjoy seeing?

- How alive and well is your mojo?

- How balanced does your life feel?

You can download your personal version of this checklist by visiting http://paulluen.com/documents

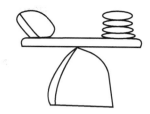

2
Rebalancing

Now you've gained some perspective and some diagnosis, maybe you've noticed how far you've unconsciously shifted away from where you began your entrepreneurial or career journey. This may feel uncomfortable, and even painful, but this is nothing to be worried about. If you'd made big plans for yourself and they haven't yet come to pass, it takes courage and strength to accept that perhaps not all is going as you had hoped. Any pain or sense of loss that you feel when acknowledging this doesn't mean that you can't turn things around, or that you can't build on the successes you've achieved so far.

I know only too well that commercial demands and pressures can be all-consuming and it's easy to lose sight of the world around us. Then something happens that stops us in our tracks; be that a family event we can't attend, the birth of a child, the death of a loved one or a missed sports day, school play or parents' evening. This makes us pause, and we realise that we're missing out on that other deep and personal sense of purpose that connects us to our families, friends and the wider community. Discovering what we've lost connection with can be frightening or shaming. I know it was for me, but still I was scared of taking my eye off my business life.

We focus most of our attention on the 'need' to keep delivering results, revenue, profits and returns to shareholders. In doing so, many of us tend to forego accountability to ourselves, our own health and well-being. We're almost running on empty, yet we continually allow ourselves to be enterprise-focused in pursuit of 'success'. The question is, 'Who's looking after the machine that drives us?' The answer is, 'No one but yourself.'

Reset

Right now, if you were standing in front of a mirror, what would that person looking back at you say with complete honesty? I encourage you to revisit the checklist at the end of Chapter One. Ask yourself those hard questions and be completely truthful with the answers. It's tough to admit that I've answered 'Yes' to many of those checklist questions. At the root of it all was a total imbalance in my life, and so many professionals fall into exactly the same trap.

When and where I ate was consistently disrupted. I frequently skipped meals, and when I did eat, it was often junk food or an unhealthy snack between appointments, because I simply didn't allow myself the time to choose or prepare healthy food. It was exhausting, but nothing stopped me from extracting the absolute maximum out of every day. Family and social events were sacrificed because of an urgent deadline or being away again on an 'important' trip.

It's too easy for life to become one constant cycle of disruption because we willingly accept it's the right trade to make; it's become the norm and we no longer challenge it. No wonder we have too little time to exercise and look after ourselves. Until, that is, the moment when we realise that all the things we used to enjoy have been eclipsed by this disruptive career and business obsession. That's not success! The irony is, if your life were a business plan, you'd never write it in such an unstructured way. The fear that drives many of us is that unless we keep up this madness, we'll fall behind and success will slip through our fingers. We lack sleep, rest and nourishment, and our business performance wanes.

It's a cumulative process of slow decay that starts to catch up with us as we make more and more poor decisions in our business and personal lives. Pressure begins to build, there's less room to flex and we become more reactive than proactive. The problem is that it all happens so slowly that we don't see it. Face it, you're almost certainly doing too much and others around you are doing too little. You're a busy fool, managing not leading. You're inadvertently diminishing your team by doing part of their jobs, allowing them to abdicate responsibility so that you carry the burden and unwittingly accept their responsibilities. That has to stop!

Reinvest

How present are you with the people you love? Have you noticed that look of disappointment on your partner's or kids' faces when you've had to let them down again, you forget to show up or you're late for a get-together? Work comes first and they come second. Have they ever told you something that's important to them, but you didn't notice because you were too busy checking your messages on your phone and only had one ear listening to them? If you haven't noticed, you can bet your bottom dollar they have.

Your family are your bedrock, and they'll do anything to support you, even if they live in the shadows. They're the ones who, if you fall, will pick you up – as they have always done, perhaps without your proper acknowledgement. We need to reconnect and reinvest in them; in doing so, we reinvest in ourselves.

We should be able to share with them our innermost hopes and dreams. We should celebrate our wins with them, and let them commiserate with us when we lose.

When a friend of mine told me his wife had caught him checking his phone as she was about to give birth, my heart sank – as did his, when he realised his life was totally out of balance. Being there physically wasn't enough, because he wasn't really present when his wife needed him most. Until I rediscovered the joy of that presence with my wife and children, that trait was costing me more than I realised. Although it was hard to begin with, my family and I spend more quality family time with each other, which I relish. When my young daughter once said to me, 'Dad, it was great you weren't on your phone,' that meant so much to me. Why? Because it reflects my deeper purpose as a human being and a parent; I do what I do so I can provide for, support and nurture my family. At the same time, I keep in mind that I also serve my clients and colleagues.

For so long, that equation had been the other way around. Today, I'm careful not to allow my business life to interfere with my family time. After all, I wouldn't begin a social call with my wife during a board meeting. I've learned to let go and say 'fuck it' to all the connectivity. As a result, my phone is configured with zero notifications and calls are almost always set to silent unless I choose otherwise. I take few calls when I'm working, and I batch my call time to suit me, so I am not interrupted.

Prioritise outcomes for others

As much as I can, I try to think from the other person's point of view, and to answer the question in their minds, 'What's in it for me?' That means everything I do is focused on achieving planned outcomes, so I front-load my thinking towards the goal. If someone wants some of my time, I ask before I respond, 'What outcomes are you seeking?' This behavioural change has massively improved my productivity and eliminated many meaningless calls and meetings when a simple exchange of information over email or text suffices. It also places the onus on the other person to 'do the work' in advance. I'm much more curious about their wants and needs. This is a big change from the 'old me', who talked more, had less empathy and was far too much 'me, me, me'.

We all have two ears and one mouth, so we should use them in that proportion. I'm naturally a people person, so I love meeting and learning from others. The most important thing in many people's lives is themselves: if you can help them talk about their challenges and what they desire, that creates opportunities to be influential and bring about positive outcomes. As I've become more mature, and by investing so much in learning, there's now more consideration behind what I say. By placing others at the centre of my curiosity, I believe that I've reconnected with my truer self.

Surrender your ego and practise humility

I've always tried to do the right thing by others, but I wish I'd discovered the true meaning of that when, in December 2007, at the onset of the global financial crisis, my business faced its greatest challenge. As Christmas approached, I stood in front of the whole of the company, knowing that 2008 was going to be tough and that I'd have to make some difficult changes. My Christmas message sent them all away telling them not to worry. Two weeks later, when I saw that the industry trade index (the Baltic Index) had lost 94% of its value in six months, reality hit home. I had to tell them I was making 25% of the workforce redundant and I was imposing a four-day week for the rest. I genuinely believed I had taken the right approach in my Christmas message, but the reality was starkly different. Two months later I began receiving feedback from the workforce, who told me they were shocked and angry I'd *not* signalled at Christmas that bad news was just round the corner. They would rather have been made fully aware of the situation, but I had assumed that putting it off would somehow be the better option. As a result of this critical feedback, I learned one of my biggest leadership lessons: what's expected most is total honesty on all occasions.

The next lesson I learned was the value in rebuilding trust by publicly and sincerely admitting that I had made the wrong call. Saying 'sorry' under those circumstances was the making of me as a leader, as it showed me the power of humility encapsulated in that one simple word. Because I like to try new initiatives without being afraid to fail, I know I will make mistakes – and when I do, I always say 'sorry', whatever the circumstances. This helps build trust and agility in an organisation, and it develops entrepreneurial thinking and controlled risk taking.

I'm also comfortable with admitting publicly when I don't have all the answers (and I never will). This has given me extra strength as a leader when trying to find solutions as part of a team. It's also increased my engagement with the people I work with, and deepened their level of trust in me as a leader. I've discovered how uplifting it is to work with humility and show vulnerability – two key human attributes. I no longer need the mask that I was hiding behind, which was fuelled by ego and covering up all sorts of issues and concerns.

Business is all about having really meaningful, deep conversations from a nurturing perspective. You need to nurture: not just your staff, but your customers, your suppliers – in fact, *everyone*. When you're consistently and unconditionally nurturing relationships that speak to the values of other people, the feedback you receive will reflect the true persona that you project, and this will nourish you further. It leads to better conversations, and you'll begin to feel better as a result.

The best investment you can make, therefore, is in yourself and in reconnecting with your story. Where there are gaps in your knowledge, understanding or abilities, make time to develop your emotional and thought capital. It's easier than ever to learn now that there are so many online resources available. Podcasts and audiobooks mean that you can learn even while you exercise, drive, wait in line, travel by train or simply when sitting and being peaceful. These tools have been transformational for me, because they allow me to consume far more content than I could by reading the written word. If, like me, you initially resist the idea of audible learning, my advice is to stick with it. It's a developing and increasingly sophisticated method of learning, and once you adapt to its style and embrace its amazing range of content, you'll begin to consume and retain the information at twice the speed of reading. Audio content also develops your listening skills and improves your conversations, as your brain becomes trained to better absorb information. As a result, you will become a more active, attentive listener and you'll be more inclined to use your mouth and ears in the right ratio.

Work on your business, not in it

I used to regularly feel exhausted by running just one business. Now, being older (and perhaps somewhat wiser), I have more energy and vigour than ever, *and* I'm running four growing businesses at the same time. Thinking about that made me curious about how it could be possible. The key is to break a series of habits and learn to do the important, non-urgent work that was consistent with my pay grade, rather than the lower value, easier, but not important stuff that most underperforming executives waste their valuable time on. These 'busy fools' get trapped in mediocrity.

Today my mantra, devoid of ego, is to *only do what only I can do*. That mantra starts with an awareness of your strengths and preferences. Once you know what these are, you can double down on such tasks and activities to keep you in 'flow', fully energised and effective. When you can make this approach a habit, you'll keep your entrepreneurial spirit alive and ascend to the higher reaches.

Be aware that this approach can wreak havoc and create a trail of chaos unless you develop your ability to delegate and invest in your capabilities as a coach. Across my businesses we practise the Challenging Coaching philosophy – high challenge with high support yielding high performance (as explained in the book *Challenging Coaching* by John Blakey and Ian

Day).[2] A historic weakness of mine was to revert to a 'Mr Fix-It' mentality when someone brought me a problem. If this sounds like you, stop solving other people's problems! Instead of inadvertently diminishing your people by accepting 'back-delegation', challenge them to gain fulfilment in finding the solutions for themselves.

In my earlier days I believed that for the business to succeed I had to run it from a top-down perspective. I thought that I had to be involved in all the decision making, because I was what the business revolved around. Anything less would have made me feel that I lacked ownership and responsibility, and that I couldn't possibly be leading effectively from the front. I thought that keeping a tight grip on almost everything represented the freedom that came with being your own boss. Freedom? Far from it. With hindsight, I now see that I'd built myself into a tightly packed structure created from my idealism and my preconceptions of what leadership looked like. The walls were of my own making, and they were literally boxing me in; like a caged bird, there was little room to spread my wings. What was the use of blue-sky thinking when I was rapidly losing sight of the sun?

Today, I couldn't be more different; I now enjoy the highest ever levels of engagement and empowerment

---

2   J Blakey and I Day, *Challenging Coaching: Going beyond traditional coaching to face the FACTS* (Nicholas Brealey, 2012)

in my businesses, and my energy is spent on only doing what only I can do. These things are:

- Attracting, developing and retaining talent in the business

- Creating the conditions, environment and systems for success

- Facilitating the definition and execution of strategy

- Disruptive, innovative 'blue-sky' thinking

- Nurturing and supporting the development of future leaders

The higher we climb up the ladder of success, the more significant are the problems we try to solve. In turn, that requires higher levels of energy and intellect. If we follow the same old path, it will stunt our ability to problem-solve.

As a result, I'm no longer chasing my own tail and I look forward to the immediate years ahead, since my focus has shifted towards creating spaces in which to thrive, pioneer and trail-blaze. I've discovered that there's more to running a business than simply running the fastest once the starting gun has fired. I'm now set up to thrive in the long term, rather than using up all my energy in the first few hundred metres until I stumble and fall with exhaustion, gasping for air as the other runners pass me by. I've slowed down to speed up, and I'm much better equipped to excel and to rise above mediocrity.

Checklist: Rebalancing

- How often do you set time aside to reflect deeply and benchmark? Is it enough?

- How happy and engaged are you and your team? Do you know?

- How invested are you in yourself?

- How hard are you working on your mindset, attitude, behaviour, rituals, connection, health and wellbeing?

- How often are you sacrificing precious time with family or friends? Who have you lost connection with?

- How comfortable are you about having challenging conversations with key people on key issues? To what extent are you avoiding these conversations, allowing false harmony?

- How much risk do you take when trying new things?

- How scared are you of failing?

- How big is your ego, and when was the last time you said 'sorry'?

- How authentically are you being your inner self, rather than complying with social norms? Dare you be different?

- How often do you solve other people's problems for them?

You can download your personal version of this checklist by visiting http://paulluen.com/documents

3

Discovering Purpose And Values

The eulogy

Imagine you're at a dear friend's funeral. The church is packed with people and so is the outside area, with mourners listening to the service over a PA system. The vicar starts to celebrate the deceased's life achievements and what they meant to their families, friends and community at large, and then you have the stark realisation that it's *you* he's talking about as you look down on the proceedings from above. What would you want people to say about you at your funeral? What would your achievements in life have been? How would you want to be remembered?

I did this exercise about fifteen years ago and it really helped me to understand that many people go about their lives in a pretty aimless fashion – back then, myself included. From that moment, I began to engage with my greater sense of purpose. Until then, my life had lacked any real, identifiable, articulated direction – as if I'd never considered it to be of any importance. Ask yourself, 'What gets me out of bed in the morning?' How clear are you on why you do what you do? For far too long, I didn't have a clue! Perhaps the word 'purpose' itself has, well, lost its purpose in your eyes and is reduced to one of those fluffy terms that entrepreneurs like to bandy about, detached from its real meaning.

It's vital that we keep purpose front of mind; it's the cornerstone of why we exist, not only as human beings but also in respect of businesses. Purpose feeds on our source of original inspiration, the thing that fired us up the most, beyond considering what the financial rewards might bring. It's that one thing that connects you and your enterprise to the aspirations you have for your family, your friends, your colleagues and the wider community. Purpose tells us why we do the things we do. It solves the puzzle we make for ourselves, guiding us towards experiencing that priceless sense of fulfilment.

Nobody gets in a car without knowing where they're going – if they did, they'd just drive around aimlessly. It's important that we know and understand our purpose, because it anchors our existence and indicates which way 'true north' lies.

Starting out

I formed my first business after some difficult times in a previous company, five years before my 'light bulb' moment about purpose. Whether through frustration, as a kneejerk response, or perhaps an 'I can do that' attitude, I dived in head first without much of a clue about where I, or my business, was going. All I knew was that I needed to generate enough income to pay the bills. That's not much of a purpose; it was more of a need to survive. I'd given no real thought to why we existed as a business or what we wanted to do. I was unconsciously content to stumble along in the dark without any sense of direction – like many business owners, as I now realise. I know now that I'd lost sight of my sense of purpose, or perhaps never had a valid one in the first place. That was partly due to running at a pace that I wasn't able to maintain. No matter how hard I played at being the busy exec, it was little more than a performance. If I hadn't listened to some wise advice from my mentors and taken the time to slow down, I wouldn't have found that space to become curious about my life – to understand more about the wonderful opportunities (and challenges) to which I could align myself.

Understanding my own purpose has helped me understand my business purpose. My personal mission statement is *to live a fun, disciplined and adventurous 120-year life, nurturing others to live better*. It's audacious – to live to 120 is a long shot, but I'm going to give it a go, and this informs the choices that I make about my body and the habits and rituals I practise. Of course I want to have fun and adventure; the world's a big place with so much to see and do, and with friends and family I want to plunge into the most amazing, intense and emotional experiences available. The more I'm able to achieve my personal and business goals, the more I'm able to serve others. When the dots connect for you through discovering your purpose, you'll also be serving yourself with complete sincerity and integrity. That's a contagious quality.

We all recognise those leaders who are completely aligned with their purpose and desire to serve others, whatever other flaws they may have! Whether it's John F Kennedy, Martin Luther King, Mahatma Gandhi or the young Swedish environmentalist Greta Thunberg, their purposes differ but the world understands what they each stand for. Purpose creates impact and is infectious when a person is so obviously committed to it. As business leaders with purpose, there's no reason why we, in our own spheres, shouldn't be a version of those inspirational leaders. We can be similar role models who share a purpose for the common good of the business and those who work in it.

Discover your purpose

If you imagine your life as a book, you'd owe it to yourself to write an epic. With that in mind, I implore you to develop your own personal purpose statement. Invest some time in deep reflection to probe your answers to questions such as:

- Who am I?

- What do I do?

- Who do I do it for?

- What do they want or need?

- How are they changed by my actions?

Aim high when creating your statement; be true to yourself and the future you want. Never base your purpose on what you think other people would say – it's your life journey, not theirs. Don't let the mediocrity of the masses influence the epic story you're about to write or limit your impact on society. Choose words that reflect positive action. Instead of stating what you want to avoid, speak positively and reflect what you want to be, do and experience. Write in the present tense: 'I am' and 'I do', not 'I will'.

When it's done, sign it – your signature reflects your commitment to your words. Display it in a place where you will see it. Your life is a work in progress, and so should your purpose be. Accept that it may change over time. When that happens, don't fret; simply adjust your purpose statement. Feel free to adjust it iteratively as you gain clarity on the answers to each of the above questions.

When you've completed the exercise, it will no longer be your alarm clock that gets you up in the morning – it'll be your *purpose*!

Discover your values

Values are innate. They highlight what we stand for and represent our unique, individual personality. Values guide our behaviour, providing us with a personal code of conduct which delivers a sense of fulfilment when we uphold it in everyday life. Living incongruently with our values causes internal conflict and a feeling that you've done something you're not proud of. Knowing your personal values changes your behaviour for the better. There are various ways to discover your values, and it always starts with asking yourself a series of questions. Here are some examples to get you started:

- What's important to you in life?

- If you could have any career, without worrying about money or other practical constraints, what would you do?

- When you're reading news stories, what sort of story or behaviour tends to inspire you?

- What type of story or behaviour makes you angry?

- What do you want to change about the world or about yourself?

- What are you most proud of?
- When were you the happiest?

To frame your values, take a blank sheet of paper and brainstorm your answers to these questions. I've listed some words below that may help you:

- Achievement
- Adventure
- Courage
- Creativity
- Dependability
- Determination
- Friendship
- Health
- Honesty
- Independence
- Integrity
- Intelligence
- Justice
- Kindness
- Learning
- Love

- Peace

- Perfection

- Security

- Simplicity

- Sincerity

- Spontaneity

- Success

- Understanding

- Wealth

Once you've completed your list of values, prioritise them to help you get even closer to defining what's important to you.

Alternatively, check out Dr John Demartini's website (https://drdemartini.com) for a guided values discovery process. For what it's worth, and with humility, I'm pleased to share my core values with you: wellbeing, relationships, personal mastery, fitness, freedom, luxuries.

Business purpose and values

The guiding, powerful principles of purpose and values apply equally to business, and they represent business 'storytelling' at the most foundational level.

When considering business purpose and values, it's all about putting the customer at the centre. After all, the customer is the only person with the power to sack everybody in your company, directors and shareholders included, by taking their business elsewhere. Thinking in these terms encourages you to be more customer-centric. Your internal team comes next in your considerations.

Under any circumstances, putting somebody else's need above your own is a great way to live. The more we seek connection, the more we discover the impact of alignment and go beyond the pay cheque. This awareness can permeate an organisation, so everybody feels that the work they're doing is meaningful and has an impact. For example, when NASA first put a man on the Moon, the cleaner who swept the floors and emptied the rubbish at Mission Control was just as connected to the greater purpose as the engineers who designed the software and the spacecraft.

When you observe and define a sense of purpose, and you align everybody to it, you intensify engagement and accountability. It's about working towards a goal-driven plan over a defined period in which everyone involved decides on their own objectives to achieve that plan. It answers their questions, 'Why am I coming to work? What's the greater good that my blood, sweat and tears contribute to, other than my monthly salary?' Investment in the business then becomes shared, emotional capital. The enterprises that succeed and endure are the ones that have a higher sense of purpose with an internal culture that fuels their purpose.

Brands with inspiring purposes

Who	Vision, purpose or mission statement
Amazon	Mission: 'We aim to be Earth's most customer centric company. Our mission is to continually raise the bar of the customer experience by using the internet and technology to help consumers find, discover and buy anything, and empower businesses and content creators to maximise their success.'[3]
Facebook	Mission: 'To give people the power to build community and bring the world closer together. People use Facebook to stay connected with friends and family, to discover what's going on in the world, and to share and express what matters to them.'[4]
Tesla	Mission: 'To accelerate the world's transition to sustainable energy.' Vision: 'To create the most compelling car company of the twenty-first century by driving the world's transition to electric vehicles.'[5]
Nike	Mission: 'To bring inspiration and innovation to every athlete in the world.'[6]

3 'Our Mission', Amazon, www.aboutamazon.co.uk/uk-investment/our-mission
4 'Facebook Investor Relations FAQs', Facebook, https://investor.fb.com/resources/default.aspx
5 'About Tesla', Tesla.com, 'https://www.tesla.com/en_GB/about
6 https://about.nike.com

Make it a central part of your purpose to build a company where everybody feels engaged, fulfilled and rewarded in serving the customer. This will give you the greatest probability of success in achieving your business and personal goals. It will help inform your most critical agenda, which is all about attracting, developing and retaining talent, the only enduring source of differentiation in any business. Products and services you can imitate and copy, talent and culture you can't. That's why it's far better to create a culture that encourages a three-way, organic conversation between the business, its talent and the customers. They are inextricably linked, and successful enterprises recognise that this stems from a clearly defined sense of purpose. Where that definition is lacking, it's near impossible to inspire talented people to excel on a business's behalf, because they aren't aligned or don't share a common purpose. In that case, the most rewarding aspect of being employed will be getting paid at the end of the month, without any care for what the business stands for – because the business hasn't defined what that is. It's no use blaming the employees; where there is no real purpose, there is no loyalty, no efficient productivity, no meaningful customer interaction and, ultimately, no growth.

Since I discovered purpose, I have implemented it into one of my own businesses from the earliest stage. I believe this has been central to its success. The company exists 'to revolutionise organisations using drones'. When we recruit, we sell our mission to revolutionise and disrupt the market, because the most energetic and engaged of people we want to hire like to think of themselves as revolutionists.

The long-term vision we share (to deliver £3 million net profit by 2023) is that we're a great company where everyone feels connected, valued, fulfilled and rewarded. As each year progresses, we're scaling up to achieve that. We're landing our own 'men on the Moon' every day. Everyone in our business participates in its equity and growth, and each one can see how that becomes a reality though their efforts. Our people work long, smart and hard in pursuit of that financial goal, because they understand how it is driven by purpose. Each one of us at every level can, therefore, answer the question 'What's in it for me?' Part of purpose is to answer that question from your employees' perspective. In a near full employment market, any job applicant will be asking themselves the same thing, so it's even more important to tell your story and advocate your purpose in any vacancy you advertise if you want to attract the right talent.

Strategy follows purpose

When I mentor executives or owners of small- and medium-sized enterprises (SMEs), it's noticeable how they generally clam up when I ask them to sum up their strategy in thirty seconds. They seem embarrassed if they can't really say, or if they struggle and make a garbled attempt. I empathise with them because I know that if they haven't found their real purpose, speaking their strategy out loud will always be a hard task. Unless they've engaged with purpose, or had mentoring, they *will* struggle to gain clarity on what their strategy is. If they don't know what it is, how will anyone else in their organisation know what they should be doing to develop and grow the business? In which case, how will that business ultimately survive? Knowing what the strategy is must be a fundamental part of any business leader's job, so knowing its purpose is key to the business's survival. None of this is possible unless you first understand who you are serving.

It also needs to be a team game, in which the business owner or leader co-curates the resultant strategy. Winning the hearts and minds of the people you work with is vital for winning the hearts and minds of your customers. There's no point in employing a top-down, hierarchical decision-making process that imposes a strategy without everyone being on board and involved. Instead, create a complete ownership around the mission, the vision, the values and then the strategy. As humans, we innately perceive the need to be in control, giving us a desire for ownership. When that ownership is shared, there's no room for anyone to say they disagree. Ownership of a shared strategy and vision is difficult to walk away from.

Back when I wanted to be in control of my own destiny, with my fingers in every corner, it never occurred to me that strategy could be co-curated and contribute significantly to the success of the business. I was wrong. Some business leaders believe it's a weakness to involve other people in the company in this process. I beg to differ, because all too often there is still too much ego involved in business at the leadership level. Where some leaders think that the decision making is their prerogative alone, I would say it's the leader's responsibility to create the conditions for success. Of course, it's important how a team is selected to facilitate the definition of the strategy, and these should always be those who are the most reliable and responsible, with the knowledge and the wisdom, who you respect and trust.

Checklist: Discover your purpose and values

- What's your purpose?

- How clear are you on your values?

- Why does your business exist?

- What is its long-term vision?

- Is it emotionally compelling?

- Is it expressed in the eyes of the customer?

- How aligned is the organisation, if at all, on that?

- To what extent have you involved the key people in the business in curating your long-term vision?

You can download your personal version of this check-list by visiting http://paulluen.com/documents

4

Winning The Talent War

One of my strongest beliefs is that the only enduring sources of differentiation in any business are *people* and *culture*. That's why my top annual priority always focuses on attracting, developing and retaining the best talent to develop a cult-like culture. Every business needs to recruit from that top 10% of 'A-players', and to do that, you've got to win the talent war.

I've long learned that as a leader, making the right decisions about who to recruit isn't just a matter of looking at a CV. Putting right my errors of judgement has cost me a lot of time and money. In this chapter I will share the recruitment process that we now use in all my businesses, which I'll look at from two distinct perspectives: the business and the applicant.

If we didn't need people in our businesses, everything we did would be performed by artificial intelligence. Thankfully, we've not yet reached that point and the human factor remains critical in every area. The philosophy is simple, yet it's so powerful – if you look after your people, they'll look after your customers, who, in turn, will reward your business by spending their hard-earned cash with you. Everything always comes back to people, so we need to attract the right and best people to work with us. The question begins not so much with the 'who', but the 'how'.

How attractive is your business?

With more jobs available than employees, you are competing to attract talent into your organisation. Place yourself in the shoes of a prospective employee and take a look at yourself:

- What's unique about you as an individual and as an employer?

- How does your organisation stand out from the crowd and scream 'We're the best company you'll ever work for'?

Millennials (born between 1981 and 1996) and those born afterwards aren't afraid to hold businesses up to the highest scrutiny. Loyalty to one employer is harder to come by, with employees being less averse to jumping from job to job to fulfil their needs. This means we need to work doubly hard on our employer proposition if we want to attract the best talent. That begins with clearly identifying and articulating our sense of purpose so that potential employees understand the impact of the work they'll be doing to make it more meaningful. Millennials, in particular, have a deeper need for meaning in their work, and it's our job to anchor that story in our employee value propositions. Only then can we move on to creating an attractive employee benefits package that goes beyond offering a competitive salary.

By placing ourselves in candidates' shoes, we can better answer their question 'What's in it for me?' This prompts us to think about how attractive we are to prospective employees in respect of vision, mission and values, which must underpin everything the business stands for. In my own businesses, all the 'people' decisions we make are centred on our values, fundamental attitudes and behaviours. Articulating these is a high priority when creating job advertisements.

Company show reel

Video content is one of the most successful conversion tools available to any business, and it's a powerful communicator when attracting talent. My businesses make full use of video through a series of show reels designed to create a feel for who and what the business is, using a human touch that is harder to convey in a traditional online or print advert. Video content featuring our people and extolling our values provides a snapshot of the types of people who work in the business, and reflects the business values and culture. I would encourage every business to make at least one show reel. Although a website can be a great tool, it lacks the same degree of meaningful impact as video content. It can be anything from a two-minute clip (even if shot on a smartphone) about current developments, product launches, events or achievements; each video builds credibility that this is a business worth working with. Post this content across all social media platforms and channels so the brand becomes omnipresent. You can post it in isolation or to complement an online job advert.

Advertising the job

Winning the talent war is as much about being able to tell your story as about discovering what your potential new recruits have to say about themselves. How the business presents itself from the moment you advertise a job sets the tone of who you are and what your business stands for. The example included in this section isn't so much a job description, but a company narrative that we hope resonates with applicants who feel they can be, or are, aligned with our values. For us, that's a vital first filter in attracting who we'd like to work with. We also want the job advert to actively dissuade candidates who are not aligned with our values from applying. From the applicant's perspective, our aim is to present ourselves as a company that has honesty and integrity, which they would want to work with because we share mutual values.

The following example is typical of a job advert that my businesses create to attract the best candidates for selection. We believe in being 100% transparent from the outset by clearly indicating:

- The company mission statement
- A series of outcomes we expect the employee to achieve
- The essential key performance indicators (KPIs)
- Experience and qualifications
- Critical competencies and skills
- Our core values
- Roles, responsibilities and reporting line

SAMPLE JOB ADVERT

You won't see another opportunity like this while you're trawling the job sites through bland adverts from boring companies in tedious sectors. There's no doubt that drones are changing the world and you'll probably have heard quite a lot about them over the last few months! Reports value the industry at £100 billion in the next five years – there's no sector like it for growth and opportunity. You could say the right place, the right time! We'd say, great vision.

Martek CUAS exists to *dominate* the counter drone systems market. We're seeking a dynamic, enthusiastic and hardworking sales-focused graduate who thrives on challenges and who has an ambition to become a field sales executive with more than £50,000 OTE within twenty-four months.

Our people values are G-O-L-D:

- **G**row – always learning and stretching ourselves
- **O**utwork – we're relentless, resilient and think 10x
- **L**everage – always amplifying remarkable assets
- **D**isrupt – inventive, ingenious and trailblazing

We also offer you the truly unique chance to join in the success of this amazing scale-up by acquiring shares in the company. This means you have the opportunity to earn six-figure sums from future business value. Your hard work *will* be rewarded in spades.

The role will develop around the successful applicant, but there will be core activities you will be involved with:

- Creating, chasing and closing opportunities in superyacht and critical infrastructure sectors
- Delivering world-class *wow* moments to clients and prospects while having fun
- Attending superyacht and counter drone exhibitions across the world in a 'millionaire's playground'

Essential personal traits and skills:

- Self-starter with sales experience

- First-class communication skills
- Intrinsically motivated with a growth mindset
- Energetic
- Can-do, will-do attitude
- Hardworking and committed to working long, smart and hard
- Resilient
- Creative problem-solver

What we offer:

- Strong vision, mission, values and leadership
- Amazing training and development opportunities for advancement
- Great place to work with a good social scene
- Flexible working and holidays
- Westfield Health and subsidised gym
- Perkbox membership (offering various discounts)
- Free breakfast, tea and coffee

You will be based in Leeds city centre with a starting salary of up to £25,000 per annum + bonus £6,000 per annum and a share scheme. To apply, forget about sending us a boring CV!

Please visit our website to complete a quick test, then email us to confirm:

- You've taken the test
- Your record of % achievement of your sales targets
- A two-minute video selling yourself to us.

We can't wait to hear from you.

How does that compare to what you're used to seeing?

Where to find candidates

The process of recruitment has been disrupted over the last few years, and our standard approach now is to use online job boards like Indeed, Total Jobs, CV-Library and Monster. I also use targeted searches on LinkedIn, which has some cool automated outreach tools – well worth a look if you're not familiar. That said, our policy is 'grow your own' and to promote from within, rewarding total alignment with our culture and values. My experience shows this to be an effective, lower-risk strategy than bringing in somebody new. I'd rather invest in upskilling a hungry and valued existing employee than bring in a newbie with so-called experience. Knowledge and skill can be trained, but attitude and behaviour can't.

Recommend a friend

Our success rate has been huge in hiring people through our existing employees' networks. It's an incentivised programme that rewards the referrer with £1,000, paid once the new recruit has successfully completed their probation. Nobody is tempted to recommend a friend they believe won't, or can't, live up to our values and high-performance culture. Employees are extra careful and make a massive preselection judgement before they introduce anybody to the business.

Agencies as a last resort?

My experience of recruitment agencies has been consistently poor. These days, I consider them to be little better than parasitic postal workers. The problem is, in my opinion, that few agencies are anything better than highly motivated salespeople who put forward any candidate to fulfil a daily quota without any real degree of selection. What's more, they charge a whopping 20% of starting salary costs if they successfully place a candidate, irrespective of whether the candidate stays.

When considering an agency, stipulate from the outset the criteria for pre-filtering in advance, similar to the specific attributes I've described above. On that basis, it shouldn't be unreasonable to expect the agency to pre-interview their filtered candidates before sending them on to the business, along with supporting evidence. The agency's fees should also be refundable if any candidate fails to complete their probation period. If the agency is not prepared to negotiate some form of contingent rebate or refund, that tells you everything you need to know about the agency. Either they're not confident in the candidates they're putting forward or they're not pre-filtering them.

If you regularly receive a speculative email from a recruitment 'professional', my guess is that they're simply scatter-gunning candidates with a generic narrative: 'I've got this exceptional candidate that would be great for your business.' When you ask, 'What makes them exceptional?' the likelihood is you'll never hear from them again, because they lack integrity.

Far better, in my view, are the online recruitment platforms mentioned earlier who do some of the filtering for you. If you invest time and effort in creating your profile, sharing your values and mission and posting updated employee reviews about what working for your business is like, you can hire the talent direct.

Filtering the applicants

CVs are a waste of time at the first stage of recruitment and are mind-numbingly tedious to review. In general, they're also packed with deletions and distortions of the truth. It's too easy for lazy applicants to carpet-bomb any job ad that takes their fancy with their work of poetry and fiction that they call their CV. Can you tell I don't bother with them now at the first stage?

Instead, in the job ad I frame the top six *outcomes* we need the role to deliver and ask candidates to describe (and evidence) the competencies and attributes they possess to deliver them. It's a quick and easy filtering stage. I've found that I now receive fewer, but higher quality, candidates who meet our criteria based on the values we select from. This step requires more effort than CV carpet-bombing and is powerful in separating the wheat from the chaff, saving you oodles of time.

I also ask candidates to provide a short video clip (three minutes maximum) because it's an instant way to see, feel and hear who they are. I'm looking for energy and engagement, particularly given that we're about business-to-business (B2B) disruptive innovation so the people we hire need to stand out. That, I would say, is an essential quality for any entrepreneurial business or department that's looking to scale and grow. If an applicant shows they're energetic and bright, the subconscious response makes a pretty quick judgement on whether they're going to share the same values and if they're going to fit. Over time I've come to rely on this gut feeling as a strong indicator of success with people.

Video is a natural medium for a people-focused business, and it solves half the battle in the early stages of recruitment. It's not how candidates look, it's how they come across; what are their inner attributes, and do they have energy? You can gauge a lot from a video clip (even if shot on a smartphone) and it can immediately make you want to meet that person. Even if they don't have the relevant experience, you'll get a sense that they might be someone you can help develop and nurture. A CV will never express that. Making that video will be the first test of understanding how resilient a candidate is, and resilience is one of the attributes I prioritise for all employees and team members.

After this first filter stage, I favour a process of rigorous, multi-level testing, ongoing interviews and work-based assignments before taking any decision to hire. During this, we continue to sell the dream, but we're also honest that it's not always plain sailing. Applicants are left in no doubt that they'll be expected to work long, smart and hard and to continually show resilience. If they want it they'll pull out all the stops, because once they step through the door there's no hiding place. If they fall out of the process, we've dodged a bullet.

Resilience

Resilience is a must-have asset in all employees if you're going to succeed and endure. There's no sugar-coating that business is tough; it's a hard, unfair world out there. If you can consistently find and secure resilient people, you're on to a winner – in today's 'snowflake' society, they're becoming fewer and further between.

I make no attempt to disguise the fact that candidates will be embarking on a hard journey with us, with bumps along the way. This results in some natural attrition in that we lose candidates throughout the recruitment process. Far from being disappointed, we welcome attrition, even if the candidate seems to be a good fit on face value. Make testing for resilience a key aspect of your recruitment. Ask for examples of where they've shown resilience in their business and personal lives:

- Probe deeply about real difficulties they've faced and how they stayed the course.

- Ask for examples of the most challenging things they've encountered.

- Observe their body language under intense questioning.

Don't short-cut this step under any circumstances. Your own resilience will be tested continually in the course of your career, and you need to be surrounded by people who can dig in with you and rise to the challenges you'll encounter.

Threat of reference checking

This is a powerful but subtle filter for candidates. At the start of the process, in my businesses we make clear that we will choose to speak with their previous managers. We frame this simply by asking, 'When we speak with your previous manager or direct reports, what will they say about you?'

We don't place any value on written references. If we choose to seek a reference, we'll call the candidate's previous employer and ask a series of intelligent questions, which may uncover some realities about them. When we ask the employer to score a candidate out of ten on any attribute, any score of seven or below is a big red flag. Their response might prompt us to ask for further clarification, to rule out the candidate immediately or to move on to the next stage. It's rarely the answer to the first question that matters most; it's when we ask, 'If you were to pick one criticism of them, one area needing major improvement, what would it be?'

The threat of reference checking works in a number of ways. Firstly, it ensures that a candidate is more likely to answer with real integrity. Secondly, those with anything to hide will soon vanish from the recruitment process, or you'll notice those small non-verbal communication clues that will give them away.

You can download a reference check template from http://paulluen.com/documents

Testing competence

An integral part of the recruitment process in my businesses is a work-based assignment that tests a candidate's competence for the role. The question is how to set a task that's analogous with the job they're applying for. For example, when we're recruiting for a marketing role and we need a particular campaign to be designed, we invite the candidates to present their solution. This serves two purposes:

1. It allows them to showcase their knowledge and skill, the result of which may, or may not, deliver some value for the business.

2. We receive valuable, objective and unbiased critiques and recommendations.

It's important that this competency testing is carried out with the utmost integrity, and with candidates who understand and relate to the rationale that lies behind it. This manages their expectations of what it's like to work with you and clearly shows that you value candidates' input at this level. This process sets the tone for their collaboration with you from the word go.

Psychometrics and scorecards

I place great emphasis on matching personality types to the right role. For example, it wouldn't make sense to hire somebody whose life is all about compliance and stability for a sales role. Equally, anybody who's extrovert and a highly dominant, charismatic character, wouldn't be right for a compliance or analysis role. We use two highly effective tools for our analysis: the Thomas International Personality Profile Assessment, and Wealth Dynamics. They help get people in flow, doing things that they naturally enjoy and are good at.

This in turn informs the central job scorecard, which lies at the core of all our people policies.

The job scorecard is effectively an embellished job description. It outlines the key outcomes and KPIs of the role, which drive what type of person we're looking to recruit. The trick is to work backwards:

- Gain clarity on the job scorecard.

- Drive the psychometrics based on the scorecard criteria.

- Finally, frame the job ad.

I wish I'd known about this earlier in my career, as I've made a lot of mistakes where candidates aced an interview, only to turn up on the day and decide the job wasn't for them, or vice versa. Since including psychometrics and scorecards as part of the recruitment process, I've found that we hire more of the right people, more of the time.

You can download your personal version of our job scorecard by visiting http://paulluen.com/documents

Virtual talent

Any business can massively increase its talent search by hiring virtual staff. There's a fantastic pool of talent in Asia, located in low-cost economies that are short of work and eager to plug any gaps. This is not about exploitation; it's about opportunity, through which a business can grow, embracing the global digital economy. Across my businesses I employ a considerable pool of people who have been recruited from, and live, abroad. They are treated and valued in the same way as my UK staff and are engaged in carrying out similar marketing, sales, social media, finance and admin tasks. Once they become part of the team, the benefits are mutual. The ability to search for talent across a wider geographical area, when a role doesn't require the person to physically be in the office, opens up greater opportunities to find the most resourceful individuals. This can also be particularly useful for specific, often one-off, specialist tasks for which you can seek singular experience or skills. The recruitment process is similar, with minor variations to allow for time differences and not being able to attend interviews in person.

Checklist: Winning the talent war

- Is attracting, developing and retaining great people in a great culture your number one priority?

- How well-positioned is your business to attract the best people?

- Do you actively 'grow your own' and promote from within to refine an awesome culture?

- What do your online employee review ratings read like?

- Do you encourage your team to recommend friends or family who could be your next stars?

- Are you trapped by employment agencies sending you a stream of poor candidates, and paying a fortune for the privilege?

- Are you paralysed by the process of mind-numbing CV-sifting, so you despise recruitment?

- How effective is your selection procedure in testing competence and job outcomes?

- How clear are you on what you really want from each role advertised and the key candidate attributes that will deliver the same?

- Are you taking advantage of virtual talent?

You can download your personal version of this check-list by visiting http://paulluen.com/documents

SUPERSTAR

5

Develop And Retain Superstars

Once you've attracted the right talent, this is where your real work starts. It's now all about setting people up for success to create an environment where they feel secure and supported from day one so they can thrive and grow. You need a culture of high support and high challenge with a focus on personal responsibility. Set people off with clear direction, a loose framework with clear objectives and then get out of their way as they work their magic.

Pre-boarding

After our selection procedure, and once a candidate accepts our offer, we go into overdrive to engage our new recruit with our culture. This pre-boarding process is always a pleasant surprise for candidates, which helps to ease any second thoughts on their part and accelerates a smooth transition into being a high-performing employee.

For new managers, we provide familiarisation days within their notice period. This gives them the opportunity to meet their new colleagues and ask questions about the business and the leadership team. We also invite them to social events, so they can meet their colleagues in a more relaxed setting. We send a steady stream of induction information to accelerate knowledge transfer, and we provide reading lists and podcast suggestions to get them quickly aligned with our learning culture. Often, we ask them to do a specific job-related task while working their notice period so they feel they're contributing from day one.

Everything we do before a new employee starts is geared towards setting them up for success and ensuring that their preferences are taken care of, from their IT requirements to providing a mug with their name on it. Before their official start date, we issue a company-wide announcement about who they are, their personal 'bio' and what role they'll be performing. The day before they start, their new manager makes a personal call to welcome them, build further rapport and take them through the schedule for the day ahead. New starters come in at 10am on their first day so we have time to double-check everything is ready for them. On arrival, they're greeted warmly and welcomed like a new family member so that they immediately feel comfortable. If it's a senior employee whose husband, wife or partner has clearly influenced their decision to join us, we'll send them a gift so that they too feel the warmth of the organisation.

On-boarding

Our on-boarding process of orientation and ongoing training promotes the ethos, history and traditions of the business. For the first thirty days, new employees are expected to email their direct line manager every day with:

- What they've learned

- What challenges they've faced

- Any questions

This, in addition to frequent informal conversations, helps the new employee to:

- Anchor what they're learning

- Articulate and think about any challenges

- Seek any support they need

We've found that this systemised approach not only helps employees to perform from the early stages, but is a powerful way to retain employees. The first five days are critical for helping the new employee feel that they're winning and contributing to the business, and for each of us to measure their progress. It's induction through nurturing, unlike more traditional corporate processes, which often lack energy or real purpose and don't put people at the centre. Our approach is designed to create a lasting, bespoke first impression from day one. It enables knowledge transfer, establishes the rhythm and energy that's needed to succeed in the business, and embeds a culture of lifelong learning.

Probation

Let's assume that you've executed the world's best recruitment process and have on-boarded your new employee in a truly legendary way. That must mean you're 100% certain that you've hired a superstar, right? Unfortunately, this isn't always so. Even the best recruiters in the world get it wrong some of the time.

There's 'nowt so queer as folk' and once the honeymoon period is over, people start to reveal their true character – their real attitudes and behaviours. In my opinion, a candidate will reveal their true self within six months, so we have an extended probation period to cover that period. I used to offer a standard three-month probation period, but over the years, I've seen plenty of masks slip later down the line. From a practical perspective, it takes at least three months for a new employee to get into their own rhythm in the business, to understand the culture and begin meeting expectations in full.

If there are still doubts about a new person after six months, we may extend the probation if we've seen enough cultural alignment to continue to invest in developing their knowledge and skill. That might sound counterproductive, given what I've described above, but as long as we're specific and transparent in our reasoning, I feel this justifies any extension so that the employee can work on any areas of their performance that need improvement.

In reality, this scenario rarely occurs because if we've really made a wrong decision to hire, it becomes apparent in the first four weeks. Under those circumstances, it tends to be the employee who votes with their feet. The following regular check-ins with the new employee are key for monitoring this:

- The three-point email to their direct line manager (see 'On-boarding') for the first thirty days

- Weekly one-to-ones with each leader

- Providing ongoing clarity on their role, KPIs and future tasks

Recruitment is one of the hardest tasks for any business. The art of its success lies in engaging with emotional intelligence so that the recruiter can spot the non-verbal communication signals during interview. The science is the psychometrics, the testing and the work-based selection assignments. In combination, this art and science is designed to continually increase the level of A* talent that is attracted to your business. It's not a process that any employer should be scared of; it's to be embraced, because it acts as an insurance policy. What frustrates me as a mentor is that most businesspeople are under-invested in the rigour, design and execution of the process. Ignore these at your peril, because you will run the risk of bad hires, cultural misalignment, underperformance, lack of rhythm and, ultimately, poor retention rates.

Cost of bad hires

Hiring the wrong people costs an organisation a damn sight more than most people think, in tangible and intangible ways. Most human resources professionals don't know their average cost per failed hire, and recent research from the USA shows that:

- The cost of a bad hire can reach up to 30% of the employee's first-year earnings, according to the US Department of Labor[7]

---

7   M Stevenson, 'Bad Hiring Costs – By the Numbers', HR Exchange Network, January 2020, www.hrexchangenetwork.com/hr-talent-acquisition/articles/poor-hiring-costs-by-the-numbers

- 74% of companies that admit they've hired the wrong person for a position lost an average of $14,900 (about £11,500) for each bad hire, according to CareerBuilder[8]

The effect of bad hires can be much further reaching than their high costs. They contribute to reduced morale and decreased teamwork, and this can lead to other employees making the decision to leave the organisation. If an organisation has a consistently high employee turnover, this can damage its reputation as word spreads. The statistics around bad hiring are staggering. For example, a study by Leadership IQ found that 46% of newly hired employees will fail within eighteen months.[9]

The key lesson is to invest everything you can into the whole process of attracting, developing and retaining talent.

Responsibility and freedom

It's my policy to hire talented grown-ups and treat them that way. Give them just too much to do (never too little), the right tools to work with, and an appro-

---

8   'How much is that bad hire costing your Business?', Career Builder, December 2017, https://resources.careerbuilder.com/recruiting-solutions/how-much-is-that-bad-hire-costing-your-business
9   M Murphy, 'Why New Hires Fail (Emotional Intelligence Vs. Skills)', Leadership IQ, March 2015, www.leadershipiq.com/blogs/leadershipiq/35354241-why-new-hires-fail-emotional-intelligence-vs-skills

priate balance of support and challenge – then get out of their way to let them get on with it. It's up to them *how* to deliver the key outcomes for the role – self-determination is a key motivator for all human beings. I call this our 'responsibility and freedom' culture.

This extends to the hours they work, the pattern of working they choose to adopt, and the number of holidays they take. Their choices are caveated by one critical principle – that ultimately, they deliver the outcomes required of the role. Those may include meeting service level agreements, delivering sales quotas or meeting minimum standards of performance. Allowing people a degree of freedom to deliver results lets them know that they're the ones who are responsible and accountable, which increases the level of ownership of the goals and so drives improved execution.

In reality, many of our employees prefer the structure of the traditional working week. The advantage is that they don't have to worry about not being able to attend their child's school play, keep a medical appointment or take an afternoon out every now and then. When employees are handed the responsibility and freedom to set their own objectives, they feel empowered and can claim ownership of their personal lives without any detrimental impact on their professional lives. It also shifts the business structure away from a top-down controlling leadership and creates further nurturing opportunities for employees to own their results. In this environment, people work together on a far deeper level of engagement. They are more willing to step in, in the knowledge that someone will do the same for them, without being asked to do so.

Major companies like Netflix and Virgin have been doing this for years, and this type of culture is now an irresistible trend.

Continuous professional development

If you want to maintain differentiation, your organisation needs to commit to placing continuing professional development (CPD) at its heart. It's not a luxury, it's an absolute necessity. If you ignore it, you'll soon be disrupted and overtaken by your competitors.

The CPD culture in my businesses starts at selection, where we ensure anyone joining us has a certain level of curiosity, openness and growth mindset. We set the expectation from day one that everyone does at least forty hours of CPD a year – it's non-negotiable. Most people exceed this, and we generally average over eighty hours per person each year. I do at least 600 hours of CPD annually reading 60–70 books a year, because I'm a firm believer that you can never earn beyond what you learn. If that resonates with you, embrace it and catapult your career forward.

In any organisation, there must be a balance between manager-directed and self-directed CPD for it to be most effective. Everyone has different learning styles and these need to be considered when choosing what to learn, and how to learn it. Here are some examples of what we promote and offer:

- Internal courses run by our staff, including trained trainers

- Internal training courses run by hired specialists

- Formal certified external training courses

- Unlimited free books for everyone – hard copy and audio

- Podcasts

- Blogs

- YouTube – you'll find videos on pretty much any subject you want to learn

- Webinars

- E-learning platforms

While the focus of CPD is generally on professional development, we're also keen to help our employees improve personally. We've worked with external specialists to deliver sessions on topics such as nutrition, finance, health and wellbeing, and resilience.

It's easy to *ritualise* learning. For me, learning isn't a short-term tactic or a fad – it's a lifestyle choice. It's nourishing, energising and uplifting. The more I learn, the more I realise how little I know and the more knowledge I want to acquire. I'm always curious about how, and why, things happen in a business, and how people adapt (or adopt) certain attitudes, behaviours and rituals. My focus is in seeking first to understand, and then to be understood.

When it comes to learning resources, my biggest breakthrough was discovering the wealth of material available in audio format, such as podcasts and audio books. Before that, I was somewhat sceptical about audio content because I didn't think I could assimilate it in the same way as I could through reading. When a mentor of mine told me that it was possible to consume audio books at twice the speed of reading, I thought they must be having a laugh. Within six months I was a convert, and now I can consume so much content that every day my mind is filled with amazing new ideas.

My advice to any leader is to make the effort to invest in working on yourself, because it's one of the most critical investments you'll make. According to a Chinese proverb, 'The best time to plant a tree was twenty years ago; the second-best time is now.' In other words, no matter what you've done in the past, the best time to start your learning journey is today. Lacking the time to do so is no excuse now that you can listen to summaries of books on platforms such as Blinklist or Soundview. You can consume audio content while you're walking, driving, at the gym, on a train or on a plane. I challenge anyone who believes they have no time to find the time; CPD is an integral element of your role as a leader.

Thanks to developing a culture of lifelong learning in my businesses, our results and profits have accelerated and many of our employees tell us it's changed their lives. They genuinely seem happier, healthier, fitter, stronger, more resilient and more fulfilled. Their lives have been enriched, professionally and personally, in areas ranging from mindfulness to health and wellbeing.

As a leader, it's important to spend more time investing in yourself and being open to learning and curiosity because you are the one who will inspire your employees to excel and the business to grow as a result. Learning isn't just about holing yourself up in an office, either. I like to get right into the heart of the shop floor so I can chat with my teams and be curious about what's happening in their personal and professional lives; often the best ideas come from those right at the coal face. Surrendering your ego when you're in a leadership position might sound counterintuitive but take it from me, it's one of the best decisions you'll ever make. It doesn't go unnoticed and it goes a long way.

Long-term incentive plan

If you don't step into your employees' shoes and ask 'What's in it for me?' you may never get to see your enterprise grow and scale in the ways you hope it will. A long-term incentive plan (LTIP) helps align employee and organisational goals. An LTIP typically includes some form of company share plan to encourage a shareholder mentality, which enhances the level of commercial thinking within teams and improves financial outcomes. It's important to make an LTIP performance-driven, where the reward is linked to objective metrics of personal and business performance. Draft it carefully; there's devil in the detail and it's easy to get it wrong.

Abhorrent annual appraisals!

Nobody enjoys annual appraisals, and they are blunt instruments. They tend to be awkward, contrived and hugely emotive. No employee should receive feedback that they're not already aware of during an annual appraisal, but this is what often happens in many companies. Despite being framed as a tool to improve engagement and performance, annual appraisals often achieve the opposite. That's why I've abandoned them and replaced them with systematic, regular, focused one-to-ones. I've known various businesses that believe one-to-ones are a distraction and a waste of time. I disagree strongly – they're where the magic happens.

It's a manager's job to nurture the hell out of every person they have in their team to deliver the operational agenda and achieve the company's strategic goals. One-to-ones are a key aspect of strategic execution and we're obsessive and formulaic about how we manage them. Management is most effective when it is done 'little and often'; the best managers ensure that every employee knows how they're doing on a daily or at least weekly basis, instead of giving them a positive or negative surprise in an annual appraisal.

Since we abolished annual appraisals, it's no coincidence that our people have flourished and both performance and retention have increased. I encourage you to stop wasting everybody's time on annual appraisals and instead ensure that you, and your leaders, create a structure that continually nurtures your people through weekly or monthly one-to-ones.

You can download your personal version of my one-to-one process by visiting http://paulluen.com/documents

Engagement surveys

Engagement surveys are vital for measuring how engaged your team is so that you can be certain of retaining the talent you've spent so long winning over. These surveys act as a barometer for how you're doing as an employer. I strongly believe that employee engagement is directly linked to organisational effectiveness and, ultimately, business performance. We track employee engagement each quarter by asking people to give anonymous answers on how strongly they agree or disagree with twelve questions derived from the Gallup Q12 employee engagement survey. We supplement them with three extra questions which require narrative responses:

- What's working well?

- What's not working well?

- What can you and the team do to make the things that are not working well work better? We want *your* ideas and solutions, please.

Each quarter, we share the results with total transparency. As a leadership team, we study the responses deeply and decide what we're going to act on. The feedback loop is critical in building trust and a virtuous circle of 'You said, we did'. It's now a staple in all the businesses that I lead, and my employees and leadership teams alike look forward to giving and receiving opinions and then acting on the feedback. We prioritise maintaining and improving engagement in all that we do because it's the foundation for everything else.

The adapted Gallup Q12 statements are as follows:

- I know what is expected of me at work.

- I have the materials and the equipment I need to do my work right.

- At work I have the opportunity to do what I do best every day.

- In the last seven days I have received recognition or praise for good work from someone.

- My line manager, or someone at work, seems to care about me as a person.

- There is someone at work who encourages my development.

- At work my opinions seem to count.

- The mission and purpose of my company make me feel like my work is important.

- My fellow employees are committed to doing quality work.

- I have a good friend at work.

- In the last six months I have spoken with someone about my progress.

- This last year I have had the opportunity at work to learn and grow.

Sickness

Sickness absence costs a fortune if it isn't properly managed. According to the Civil Service sickness absence data for the year ending 31 March 2018, the number of average working days lost per staff year in the public sector was 8.5.[10] I found out early in my career that self-employment is the world's best cure for sickness absence, which is one of the reasons we cap annual sickness pay at five days a year. Outside this, we give management discretion to support long-standing employees who are in real need of it, but these instances are rare. Anyone reporting in sick has to do so by phone, not by text or email, to their manager on each day of absence.

Of course, people do genuinely fall ill for all sorts of reasons, but our sickness stats have fallen to 1.4 days per employee per year. If an employee turns up for work with a genuine debilitating or germ-spreading illness, we send them straight home. Because my businesses are designed to be high-performance organisations in which employees are invested in many ways, the culture has bred peer-to-peer support and our people don't want to let others down. Duvet days simply don't exist, because nobody wins when someone else is watching *Homes Under the Hammer*. I've heard many a time 'from the horse's mouth' that in some areas of

---

10　'Health and Well-being At Work, Public Sector', CIPD, 2018, www.cipd.co.uk/Images/health-and-well-being-public-sector-summary_tcm18-41280.pdf

the public sector annual sickness days are seen as an extension of already generous annual holidays, a fact I find utterly disgraceful as a taxpayer. I'm proud of the cultures we've developed in my businesses, where the sickness rate is 80% below that of the public sector.

Return-to-work interviews

We always use return-to-work interviews when an employee comes back after a sickness absence, however long that absence may be. The main purpose is to ensure that the employee is fit to return to work and to assess if any adjustments need to be made. Best practice states that a return-to-work interview should be carried out to:

- Welcome an employee back and check they are well enough to work

- Update the employee about any changes that have taken place during their absence

- Develop, or discuss, the details of any agreed return-to-work plan

- Confirm that the employee's absence record is correct

- Allow the employee to discuss any other issues that they may need us to help them with

The mere existence of a policy of doing return-to-work interviews serves as a deterrent to employees taking occasional 'duvet days'.

You can download your personal version of our return-to-work template by visiting http://paulluen.com/documents

Exit interviews

For those who do leave our employment, we carry out a thorough exit interview in person. We're looking to learn what aspect of our management culture prompted that person to leave. All feedback is valid, because perception is reality. Over time, we've learned an awful lot from exit interviews, and made some significant changes as a result. They've highlighted areas where managers needed a little realignment or some support or clarity. Generally speaking, employees don't leave an organisation per se; they leave because of their manager. On rare occasions, an exit interview has resulted in making a small adjustment to retain a valued employee.

You can download your personal version of our exit interview template by visiting http://paulluen.com/documents

Checklist: Develop and retain superstars

- How can you improve your pre-boarding?

- How do you rate your on-boarding procedure to support new employees to succeed?

- What's your probation review process and how effective is it?

- What are bad hires costing you?

- How responsible and free are your staff?

- How do you rate your CPD culture?

- How effective is your employee development?

- Is it time to ditch abhorrent appraisals in favour of a systematic coaching culture?

- Do you have a problem with sickness absence?

- What intelligence do you gather when someone leaves?

- What do you know about engagement in your company?

You can download your personal version of this checklist by visiting http://paulluen.com/documents

6

Innovation And Intellectual Property

Now you've established a killer team in a supportive and challenging culture, the next factor that affects growth is a company's ability to truly innovate and create intellectual property in the form of highly differentiated assets. This relies on creating an innovation culture in your enterprise – something much more easily said than done.

My own definition of business innovation is simple – it's the process of monetising those light bulb moments. We all have them, but most people never act on them because they feel constrained in taking their ideas forward, fear failure or simply don't know what to do. The solution is straightforward: embed innovation into a process that you own with your team. That can be as simple as asking your salespeople to ask questions during customer visits, such as:

- What problems with current businesses or suppliers do you have that you don't have an adequate solution for?

- Which product or service causes you the most problems and why?

You could also hold quarterly team meetings where you pool ideas to answer further questions:

- What factors and conditions does our current success depend on?

- What's wrong with existing solutions to our clients' problems?

- Which of them might change over time or are already changing, putting our success at risk?

- How can we prepare for these changes so we cushion or exploit their impact?

- Who will be our customers in the future, and what will their priorities be?

- What disruptive technologies might open up new opportunities?

- Who will we be competing against in the future, and on what basis?

- Will our go-to market approach change fundamentally, and if so, how?

- What are the potential regulatory reforms?

- What assumptions must be true for this idea to be profitable?

The resulting ideas can then be tested with low-cost, low-risk experiments.

The pace of business is rapidly changing, so we must all be prepared to innovate and disrupt, or risk being disrupted. I'm all too aware when I look at my management accounts that sometimes half our revenue (sometimes more than half our profits) is derived from products or services that did not exist two or three years ago. I also know that if innovation culture was not a fundamental part of our DNA, my businesses would probably not exist, or they'd be pale shadows of themselves. Don't risk being a business casualty statistic; act now to consider what you need to do to put innovation culture centre stage.

Filtering your light bulb moments

Whether you're the innovation champion in your organisation or you've managed to sow the seeds of holistic innovation culture, chances are you'll have loads of ideas. Many of these, in all probability, will be crap – so it's important to run them through some kind of filter or stress test.

Ideas for product or service innovation fall into two categories:

1. Helps ease pain and makes someone's life easier, or reduces risk
2. Provides a sense of pleasure or emotional reward to your target audience

The next step is to assess the *scale* of opportunity available in the market. With more ideas than you have time and resources to take forward, you need to select which ideas you will develop further. You have to identify which ideas potentially offer the biggest financial returns to justify the investment risk and the distraction to business as usual. Because when you say 'yes' to an idea, you're saying 'no' to some aspect of current revenue-generating activity. These are important concepts to be mindful of.

Having completed the initial filtering stage, you now need to choose the *best* ideas to work on. How you do that is your choice. Having brought many innovations to market across various sectors and industries, I have gained enough wisdom to rely on my gut to do this. That doesn't mean I always get it right, because I don't, and failure is an important part of the innovation process. But twenty-five years' experience and an appetite for risk helps free me from 'paralysis by analysis', and I don't have an ego which is scared to fail. Depending on where you are on the risk or experience spectrum, you might want to consider things such as market analysis, focus groups and 'voice of customer' research to help signal which are the best ideas. I'd table a bet that it'll eventually come down to that simple concept of 'gut feel' anyway!

One of my guiding principles is to try a lot of stuff and keep what works. To follow it, you'll need to experiment a lot (low cost, low risk, low distraction) and accept that mistakes will be made.

Vanilla versus rum and raisin

There's nothing wrong with vanilla as a flavour. It's quite pleasant on its own, if a little bland. Place it on a counter with more colourful options, though, and it rarely gets a look-in. That's obvious when you go to one of those fancy new *gelato* ice cream parlours and there's an array of tempting desserts. I bet if you told your kids they could only have vanilla (the cheapest), they'd protest. Who in their right mind chooses vanilla in these situations? No, they'll go for the brightest, funkiest-sounding waffle-cone-topped heart attack with all sorts of nutty, sickly delights. And this'll cost you twice as much. If you take a step back and think about what it is that you're buying, it's still only ice cream. It's essentially the same product expressed in different ways to tempt you to part with more cash.

We can learn a lot from the humble ice cream, and it makes us wonder how 'vanilla' we really are.

In daily life I see so many business products as bland vanilla choices – and they wonder why they're struggling. I guess many of them lack a sense of daring to be different, but that's the only way for a business to get ahead of its competition. There's no ego attached to that, no arrogance involved – it's a crowded marketplace out there, and every business needs to step away from the pool of mediocrity and stand out from the crowd. It's easy to fall into the age-old trap of simply trying to beat the competition and exploit existing demand. By doing so, you'll have to make a cost/value trade-off decision. Do you think that's the approach Steve Jobs took with Apple? The answer is a big fat 'No'!

Whenever I'm looking to innovate a new product or service, my aim is to create or exploit some uncontested market space where I can make the competition irrelevant. This may involve creating and capturing some new or latent demand in the customer base to solve a problem within the existing competitive ecosystem. Ideally, I'm looking to break the cost/value trade-off so there's a leap in value for the customer base. This means delivering exceptional buyer utility at an attractive and disruptive price point that's accessible to the masses and delivers acceptable profit margins. It's easier said than done, but I can assure you it's possible.

One of the best examples from my experience is where we revolutionised the market in personal gas detectors on ships. These devices are used to protect workers from asphyxiation when entering confined spaces. The devices have to be calibrated at least once every six months, and back then it was conventional industry practice for ship operators to send them ashore. This was highly costly and disruptive to their organisations, because the ships would leave port before calibration was completed, which meant they needed to keep numerous spare sets. The entire logistics of getting the devices back on board as the ship moved from port to port were challenging and costly.

Our solution was to provide equipment that could be calibrated on board by the ship operator – we called it our ABC solution, Always Be Calibrated. To reduce friction in the sale of new equipment, given that ships already had working gas detectors, we offered a trade-in against their existing equipment and the facility to 'rent' the equipment. The result of this new business model was a global revolution in the calibration management of ship gas detectors, and we signed up the biggest global fleet operators. It's been one of our most successful disruptive innovations.

Positioning

Whatever intellectual property you possess or whatever innovations you're taking to market, the way you position them is critical. Positioning is simply how you articulate the key differences of your offering to the target market in a way that's emotionally compelling. It's one of the core principles of advertising and helps you to stand out from the crowd. Your company brand and reputation are important but will only take you so far. What you're looking to do as you compete for attention, hearts and minds is to frame your uniqueness inside your proposition – something that no one else can claim. The unique selling point (USP) of your product or service must resonate with the target audience as a clear benefit (not a feature) and answer their question, 'What's in it for me?'

When crafting USPs, you're looking to make claims about being:

- First

- Most

- Only

- Best

Your USP should be valuable, rare, difficult to imitate and highly leverageable. Our positioning statement for our ABC system is, 'The world's first and only on-board calibration system enabling you to slash costs by 75%.' You'll see we've used bold messaging that immediately sells value.

Premium offerings with strong margins and recurring revenue

Another key consideration when deciding how to position your product or service is whether to compete on price or value. *Never* set yourself up to compete on price alone. It's a sure-fire race to the bottom, where you end up swimming in a sea of sharks. It's a road to ruin.

Instead you need to focus on premium differentiated offerings that provide unique value to customers. These offerings need to deliver profit margins that are high enough for you to continually embrace innovation and develop further value and intellectual property. Instead, think 'better' before 'cheaper'. It's easy for any competitor to sell cheaper any time they wish, but it's more difficult for them to improve the value they offer relative to your proposition.

In general, when launching new products or services I aim for a price that's 15% higher than any established competitive proposition. I've found this to be a reasonable premium, which customers are prepared to pay in return for value. On some occasions, when we've managed to establish a truly disruptive and value-added proposition, we stretch this. It's important to experiment with market-based pricing to see what the market will stand. It's not that hard to reduce the price if you've set it too high, but beware of entering a market with a price that's too low – it's difficult to increase

97

your price once a baseline has been established and a precedent set. Explore variable pricing models based on the concept of 'elasticity of demand' versus capacity. If you have more demand than you have capacity, you can easily stretch your pricing and vice versa.

In any business model that you're advancing, look out for opportunities to create recurring revenue. A mistake I made early on was to launch products and services that did not need customers to be in touch with us after the sale. Examples of where you can 'engineer' recurring revenue into your business model include:

- Consumable spare parts, where you control the supply

- Annual licensing costs

- Annual performance test requirements

- Recurring or refresher training requirements

- Annual maintenance requirements triggered by automatic signals – think car servicing alarms on your dashboard

- Subscription-based business models, where clients have access to your product or service rather than ownership – think software-as-a-service (SaaS) business models

Fail fast!

Innovation is a tricky business; if it was easy, everyone would be doing it and blazing a trail. It's difficult because it's wrought with uncertainty. Whenever you're trying something that hasn't been done before, there's no precedent to rely on to derive any predictions from. That's what makes it such an exciting and daunting prospect.

Just because you or your market research team thinks it's a good idea, that doesn't mean that customers will part with their money to embrace your innovation. Within our innovation programmes, we tend to think along the lines of J-curves.

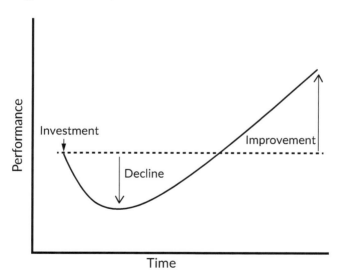

The J-curve of investment

J-curves follow distinct phases after investment: decline; improvement; returns.

- **Decline** – during this phase it's all about researching the idea and getting to a minimum viable product so you can start selling.

- **Improvement** – at this stage you start to see positive returns from sales, which are accumulating faster than you're spending money on developing the innovation.

- **Returns** – this starts when you've recouped your initial investment from sales and now you're starting to see accelerating returns from increased sales.

The reality of most J-curves is that the depth of the decline phase and the time taken to reach a point of inflection before the improvement phase are often over-estimated. I've been involved in many a project where that point of inflection never comes. In my earlier years I would sometimes blindly continue with the investment phase because the business was so deeply financially and emotionally invested that I dared not admit defeat. I now know that this is the 'sunk cost fallacy', and it's cost me dearly over time. Experience has taught me that sometimes you just have to admit defeat, and knowing when it's right to do that is more of a 'gut feel' thing. I liken it to the metaphor of drilling for oil – keep drilling as long as you feel there may be a rich well of oil below the surface.

The ability to 'fail fast' and surrender your ego over stalled or doomed projects is, therefore, crucially important. I now fail fast at many projects, which allows me to test more ideas more quickly and at a much lower cost than before. This increases the probability of success across all our innovation efforts, and it preserves cash and resources so we can 'double down' the investment when we do strike oil, maximising our returns.

Portfolio of assets

This chapter has focused on building an innovation culture to deliver unique product and service intellectual property, but it's also important to extend your thinking and invest more widely across all your business assets. Each quarter, my leadership teams meet to consider how we can innovate to improve the assets we create across the following areas:

- **Content** – blogs, brochures, articles, case studies, videos, etc

- **Registering intellectual property** – patents, trademarks, etc (see the next section)

- **Processes** – any unique business processes that you execute to drive results

- **Brand** – logos, straplines

- **Recognition** – awards, accreditations, endorsements, associations, ambassadors

- **Channels** – partners, agents, distributors, affiliations

Protecting your assets

Creating unique and valuable intellectual property is the foundation of all business success. It's a time-consuming and expensive task, which is fraught with risk. An army of people will seek to cash in on your ideas the moment you successfully go to market, and they'll do everything they can to take the easy route and steal your intellectual property. Protect it with your life! Protection can take various forms (with massively varying costs) depending on the type of asset:

- **Patent** – protects **inventive ideas or processes** that are new, useful and non-obvious. Patents are what most often come to mind when thinking of intellectual property protection.

- **Trademark** – protects **words, phrases, symbols,** etc and are often considered assets that describe, or otherwise identify, the source of underlying products or services that a company provides.

- **Copyright** – protects **the way in which ideas are expressed, ie 'original works of authorship',** such as written works, art, music, architectural drawings or programming code for software.

Copyright protects your work and prevents others from using it without your permission. You automatically get *copyright* protection when you create original literary, dramatic, musical and artistic work, including illustrations and photography.

Checklist: innovation and intellectual property

- How alive is innovation culture in your business?

- Are you working on enough new initiatives?

- What's your system to filter opportunities so you only work on the best ones?

- How disruptive is your thinking?

- How clear are you on your USPs and market positioning?

- Are you competing on price or value?

- How differentiated are your products and services?

- Are your margins strong enough to sustain and grow?

- Do your products and services generate recurring revenue?

- Are you comfortable with failing fast?

- What projects should you stop investing further in?

- How strong is your portfolio of assets?

- Are your key intellectual property assets protected?

You can download your personal version of this check-list by visiting http://paulluen.com/documents

7
Marketing

Your challenge now to achieve business success is to ensure that your value propositions are seen far and wide, in the most emotionally compelling way, by the widest possible audience. I call it the A^2 principle:

Success = Assets x Audience (A^2)

Marketing is your ability to tell stories that stir your audience's emotions so they engage with you. We're the only species on Earth that connects with each other through stories, and that's one of the reasons we've become the dominant species on the planet. One of the most powerful books I've ever read in my life is *Sapiens: A brief history of humankind* by Dr Yuval Noah Harari, which provides a fascinating insight into this concept.[11] It's an absolute must-read, and it changed my perspective on life.

We all tell stories, whether they're about what's happened in our working day, a night out with friends, or any other aspect of our life and experiences. Funny, sad, exhilarating storytelling is a part of our DNA. Too often in business, though, storytelling is missed or lacks the emotion it needs to really connect with the audience. Across my businesses, our marketing strategy is about creating remarkable imaginative narratives that speak to our audience at a highly emotional level, whatever product or service we're selling. This is where our E^3 storytelling principle comes to the fore:

E^3 storytelling = Educate, Evangelise, Entertain

Educate – providing new insights or knowledge is a sure way to capture an audience whenever we're bringing disruptive new propositions to market. It's key to helping the audience understand what's in it for them.

Evangelise – new products or services need evangelists to throw their weight behind them with a high level of passion and zeal; when it is done properly, customers can feel this passion and are positively influenced by it. Evangelising is a powerful tool in any marketer's kit.

11   Y N Harari, *Sapiens: A brief history of humankind* (Vintage, 2015)

Entertain – who doesn't like to be entertained? In the crowded field of B2B marketing, you'll rarely see content framed around entertainment – so when you manage to get this right, it's so easy to stand out. Few people are natural entertainers, which is why I find entertaining storytelling perhaps the hardest to get right.

For an example of marketing content that transcends the E^3 principle, please watch our YouTube video 'Child's Play' which is designed to show the value impact of our defibrillator product.[12] The context is that if Daddy is on a ship fifteen days away from home and he has a heart attack, he's going to die, but with our defibrillator that's child's play to use (just as if it were a Fisher-Price toy) he'll survive. A metaphor like this can be a powerful device and can subconsciously embed learning that could be resisted or is missing.

In the next sections I'll explain more specifically the strategies and tactics we use to ensure our intellectual property assets are seen and heard by the widest possible audience, using the A^2 principle to maximise business success.

---

12 Martek Marine, *LIFEFORCE Marine Defibrillator – Making saving lives child's play* [YouTube video], February 2009, https://bit.ly/39oNimU

Specialist talent

Marketing in the digital age changes faster than any other aspect of business. What worked twelve months ago may not work today. The algorithms that are the foundation of Google and social media are updated many times over, and tactics that once kept you ahead of the competition may soon leave you trailing behind for no apparent reason.

To maintain competitive advantage, you need to create and continually refine a winning team of specialists. The short-cut is to appoint a 'full stack' marketing agency to take care of it all for you; they'll sell you the dream of amazing results and promise you the world. Only rarely, in my experience, do they deliver what their fancy slide deck presentation promises. There are exceptions, but finding them is difficult and can prove expensive.

An alternative is to tap in to the rapidly expanding 'gig economy' through the multitude of online platforms where communities of specialists can be found on sites such as:

- www.upwork.com
- www.weworkremotely.com
- www.problogger.com
- www.dribble.com

- www.fiverr.com

- www.onlinejobs.ph

Most will allow you to search for specific disciplines. We always test specialists by giving them a small but real-life task to complete, then asking the candidate to walk us through their thought process with a written summary of the project. We've found this step to be crucial in testing a person's ability to deliver our desired target outcomes.

To build a killer marketing team, you need to consider hiring talent in all of the following disciplines if you don't have those skills in-house:

- Content writers

- Videographers

- Designers

- Conversion rate or user experience specialists

- Link-building specialists

- Search engine optimisation (SEO) or pay-per-click (PPC) specialists

- WordPress, WooCommerce and Magento developers

- Content outreach and repurposers

Content

At the core of every effective digital marketing strategy is the creation of remarkable, purposeful and *personalised* content assets that:

- Can be tailored to specific industries or uses
- Can be tailored to the specific needs or challenges of the target business
- Create specific concepts to help advance their business or careers

Earlier in this chapter I wrote about my E³ storytelling approach, which is about creating content to educate, evangelise or entertain. In making choices about how to personalise each type of content, you need to think deeply about the persona of your target customer:

- What do they do?
- What drives them?
- What are their pain points and pleasure points?
- What are their unmet needs or wants?
- Where do they hang out online?
- What device do they use?

Headlines

The headline is the most important part of your content. It's a popular refrain that eight out of ten recipients will read the headline but only two out of ten will read the rest. With that in mind, my advice is to invest more time in writing killer headlines than in the main body of text. Voice-activated searches have become more popular, so I'd also advise including natural spoken language in your headlines to get the best possible results from your content. The following examples adopt different approaches to targeting potential customers:

- **Direct** – goes straight to the issue or sales proposition without any attempt at cleverness: 'Kitchenware – 30% off until 30 May'.

- **Indirect** – more subtle, to pique curiosity: 'Could this be the next big thing in home security?'

- **News announcement** – which also delivers value to the reader: 'Exclusive preview of our summer range'.

- **How to** – helps the reader uncover new and specific insights: 'How to reduce survey times and costs by 52%'.

- **Question** – choose one that readers can empathise with or that they would like to see answered: 'Who else wants to get rich online?'

- **Command** – where the first word is a strong verb demanding action: 'Subscribe to *Copyblogger* today'.

- **Lists** – make them relevant to your selling proposition to help readers learn: 'Seven ways to revolutionise your business with e-learning'.

- **Client testimonials** – to provide social proof of value: 'We saved £1.6million using drones'.

Repurposing

There are abundant opportunities to repurpose your content to use across different media. The digital marketing wheel summarises the media you could use. It's up to you to select the right channel for the right message, tailored for the right audience.

The digital marketing wheel

The marketing strategy in my businesses includes a three-month rolling calendar of 'pillar' content that we deliver to support the objectives of our marketing and sales plans. Pillar content means detailed blog posts of 2,000–3,000 words that we can use as the foundation to repurpose in a multitude of forms across the digital marketing wheel. This highly effective technique gets the most out of every bit of well-researched, keyword-rich SEO-optimised content you produce. Here is a selection of tools we've used or are experimenting with to improve our content strategy:

- Infogram.com and www.Canva.com – great ways to repurpose content and turn it into infographics

- Snip.ly – lets you take posts and overlay your offer or content

- https://frame.io – allows you to leave comments over video

- https://animagraffs.com – creates animated infographics

- www.cameo.com – provides a personal famous 'shout-out'

- Amazon Transcribe – transforms your video to text

- www.rev.com – helps with captions, subtitles, etc

Audience

Let me remind you of my A^2 principle: Success = Assets x Audience. This is the final step to marketing success that enables your brand to achieve the most leverage from your remarkable, personalised content assets while reaching the widest possible audience.

A technique that's been successful across my businesses is to invest time and energy in producing a 'digital map' of everywhere your target 'personas' hang out online. This might include:

- Blogs
- Trade publications
- Trade associations
- Online forums
- Reddit
- Social media groups
- YouTube channels
- Social media influencers
- Trade show sites
- Buying portals
- Professional bodies
- Hashtags

- Podcasts

One of the best ways to share your content is through your own email list, which you should grow and refine as a strategic priority. You can also increase your audience by collaborating with people and companies that have similar audiences that lend themselves to cross-promotion.

As the world of digital marketing advances, you'll find that some pretty nifty tools emerge that can enhance the way you grow and leverage your digital audience. These include:

- www.similarweb.com – a great tool to see where your audience can be found

- www.hellobar.com – collects emails to build your list

- https://socialblade.com – provides insights to help grow your social channels

- https://influence.co – gives you access to B-list influencers

- www.dux-soup.com – helps automate your LinkedIn lead generation

- https://sparktoro.com – gives you insights into your Twitter audience

- https://vidIQ.com – helps increase the number of video views

- https://onalytica.com – connects you to influencer communities

Website

Every successful business needs an effective website. Website development is too huge a subject to cover here, and plenty of books have been written on this already. All I will say is that while it's vital to own a website that looks and feels consistent with your brand, the critical aspect of its design is that it's optimised for user experience (UX) and conversion rate (CRO). Many sites aren't, as I know from bitter experience of using them. It's commercial folly to have a site that looks and feels nice but gives visitors a poor experience with no clear 'lead magnets' or calls to action to engage with you further.

Whatever stage of maturity or development your site is at, these tools can help you improve UX and CRO:

- https://clearbit.com – a form-filling tool

- https://wordpress.org/plugins/amazon-polly – converts text to speech on-site to increase dwell time (the amount of time a user spends on your webpage after clicking a link on a search engine results page)

- https://subscribers.com – increases traffic to your website by allowing you to schedule push notifications

- www.leadquizzes.com – enables you to create quizzes that increase your leads and audience insights

- https://outgrow.co – helps you create interactive content for your website

- www.izooto.com – enables you to schedule web push notifications

- https://exitintelligence.com – helps you collect email addresses from visitors leaving your website

- www.clickfunnels.com – optimises your landing page for higher conversion rates

Automation

Some of the most transformational tools I've used over the last few years are marketing automation platforms. These help you plan, coordinate, manage and measure all your marketing campaigns, both online and offline. In my businesses, we use them in our life-cycle marketing strategy to closely manage and nurture the leads we generate so they are converted into customers faster.

So far, we've applied tools like HubSpot, Salesforce Pardot and Communigator to improve lead scoring and then run lead-nurture campaigns. The following example of a simple automated lead-nurture campaign gives more insight into the power of marketing automation:

SAMPLE LEAD-NURTURE CAMPAIGN

- Day 1 – Website personalisation persona-based offer
- Day 10 – Follow-up with introductory email
- Day 15 – Email offering new content related to first download and subsequent website activity
- Day 30 – Personal email from sales rep
- Day 45 – Email best practices whitepaper
- Day 60 – Social campaign on email best practices
- Day 75 – Website personalisation and banner ads to promote webinar series
- Day 85 – Personal email from sales rep offering a product demo
- Day 90 – Personalised ad on Facebook using targeting

I highly recommend you invest as early as possible in a marketing automation platform: when done properly, it will pay you back ten-fold.

KPIs

We systematically review our KPIs to help our marketing teams make better decisions. There are many KPIs that you can measure and manage; which you choose depends on your key challenges and opportunities. Here are a few examples:

- Marketing qualified leads

- Cost/lead

- Blog subscribers

- Email subscribers

- Downloads

- Webinar attendees

- Unique visitors to your website

- Domain authority

- Time on your website

- Bounce rate

- Likes and shares

- Follows

- Views

- Click-through rate

- Engagement

Checklist: Marketing

- How marketing-led is your organisation?

- How good are you at telling your stories?

- Are you educating, evangelising and entertaining your audience enough?

- Does your team include all the specialists you need?

- How prolific and personalised is your content strategy?

- Do you understand how critical headlines are?

- Are you using all available marketing channels for your messages?

- How well do you know your audience and how to reach them?

- What's the user experience of your website like?

- How effective is your website in converting visitors into customers?

- What marketing automation do you use?

- Are you tracking the right KPIs to reveal actionable insights?

You can download your personal version of this checklist by visiting http://paulluen.com/documents

8
Sales

Marketing attracts customers into your shop, but it's the job of the sales team to influence and persuade those customers to contract with you and, after that, to maximise their lifetime value. In many companies, marketing and sales functions often operate in silos with little interface; sometimes distrusting each other. The best companies encourage the heads of marketing and of sales to be fully aligned in terms of attracting and converting demand for products and services. Getting this right, so your leaders co-curate and execute an overall marketing and sales plan, is crucial.

Sales method

A defined sales method describes the framework, philosophy or general tactics that inform how a salesperson approaches each step of the sales process. It bridges the gap between what needs to be done and how to do it. The best sales methods turn goals into actionable steps that can be measured and monitored. Different sales methods work best for different portions of the sales process, such as qualification or discovery. Here are twelve sales methodologies to understand and consider:

1. Challenger sales

2. Conceptual selling

3. Consultative selling

4. Customer-centric selling

5. Inbound selling

6. MEDDIC (metrics, economic buyer, decision criteria, decision process, identify pain, champion)

7. NEAT selling (need, economic impact, access to authority, timeline)

8. SNAP selling (simple, iNvaluable, align, priorities)

9. Solution selling

10. SPIN selling (situation, problem, implication, need-payoff)

11. Sandler selling system

12. Value selling framework

I've found Matthew Dixon's Challenger Sale method (teach, tailor, take control) to be most effective for my businesses, and the statistics below will tell you why:[13]

- 40% of high sales performers primarily used a Challenger style.

- High performers were more than twice as likely to use a Challenger approach than any other.

- More than 50% of all-star performers fit the Challenger profile in complex sales.

Selecting your team

As I explained in Chapter Four, people are the only enduring source of competitive advantage in an organisation, and this is particularly true of sales-people. If you've ever been tempted to shorten your recruitment process and think 'good enough is good enough', you must never do that in sales recruitment. Your aim is to hire salespeople in the top twenty-fifth percentile of available talent, because I believe those people will generally perform at a level that's 100%

---

13   B Adamson and M Dixon, *The Challenger Sale* (Penguin, 2011)

above the median level of performance. Better still, and wherever possible, 'grow your own' so you're as certain as you can be that they share your values, fit your culture and have the key sales attributes. In my experience, those attributes are:

- The ability to listen

- Empathy

- Hunger

- Competitiveness

- Networking ability

- Confidence

- Enthusiasm

- Resilience

We interview our salespeople under pressure and give them a series of exercises to reveal their competence in executing their sales process. One of the first things we do is to hand them a random object, such as a pen, stapler or pair of glasses, and ask them to sell me the item. Though crude, quick and simple, it's an exercise that reveals the most about a true salesperson. To be frank, many of the 'sales professionals' I've seen over the years crash and burn with this exercise.

I complement that task with a role-play scenario where I ask the applicant to prospect, pitch and sell to me the product or service that they currently represent. Again, it's massively revealing of their true sales competence. What I'm looking for, apart from their process, is their ability to deeply engage me, to make me like them, and to see how much they're able to evangelise their product or service and sell me value. I'm also looking to see how they handle rejection and objections, and how able they are to negotiate to a close.

My end goal is to hire individuals whose skills include uncovering and meeting customers' needs first, and who have the steel to stay the course. It's well known that most salespeople give up after four rejections, so I test this too. It's not unusual for applicants to withdraw part way through the selection process, and this makes clear that we've dodged a bullet.

Sales incentives

A good, fair and well-designed bonus scheme is the perfect way to increase sales performance – almost all sales jobs come with a bonus element. You can incentivise your sales team by linking their bonus to:

- Individual performance
- Team performance
- Overall company performance
- A combination of individual and company performance

A single-factor bonus scheme will focus on a specific goal; for example, an individual employee achieving more sales. A multi-factor scheme includes other goals and is multi-layered. If the bonus is designed to target new sales, give each staff member their own targets to reach (such as a specific sales figure). Bonus schemes work best when employees can easily calculate what they are going to earn. Make sure your scheme isn't too complicated or time-consuming to administer.

Don't set targets that are either too easy or impossible to achieve. For example, for new sales a realistic target may be to improve revenue by 5–10% in a year. Consider also what bonus payment timescales are appropriate: monthly, quarterly or annually. It's often better to set short-term (quarterly) goals and make regular payments, as this is more attractive and motivating for the employee. Quarterly bonuses also allow you to evaluate what the employee is doing more often and adjust the scheme and its priorities if necessary.

The other tricky question is how much to offer as a bonus. The amount must be meaningful and 'matter' to the employee, and could be:

- A percentage of their salary

- A flat rate payment

- A percentage of their new sales

- A percentage of the gross profit from their sales

Bonuses should be uncapped to drive further sales and better performance. If you set a capped bonus for each period, once the employee has reached their target they may stop trying or slow down.

Sales planning and reporting

'Fail to plan, plan to fail', so they say – and that's why any organisation worth its salt needs to invest in quarterly sales planning. Your sales plan will inform you and your team of your objectives, tactics and target audience. The foundation of the sales plan is the set of annual or quarterly objectives that cascade down from the overall company business plan. These are usually a set of numbers and targets, such as sales revenues, contribution to gross profit and new customers. These should be realistic but challenging, matched with the resources available to deliver the plan.

Next, decide where the focus of attention will be in the market. In general, this is derived from the products you're selling and how they're positioned. Focus on the most significant and scalable opportunities, where the company has a degree of competitive advantage. Another key consideration is the maturity of the chosen sectors and their readiness to invest in your solution. Don't be too general: if you try to appeal to everyone, you'll appeal to no one.

Once you've decided on the sectors (or verticals) you'll focus on, you need to understand more about your customers' wants and needs. What are their pain and pleasure points? If necessary, revisit Chapter Seven for information about creating buyer personas. You can then build a prospect list. Digital solutions make it easy to buy in databases for specific sectors (eg from Experian) or to access online directories for prospect lists.

The final step is the most important, and that's the execution of the plan. Most plans don't fail due to major flaws in the planning, but because of weak accountability in their execution. That's where the rhythm of meetings, which we'll look at in Chapter Nine, comes into its own. That which is measured and managed gets done. Sales plans work best when they're living, breathing documents that can account for, and adapt to, anything – changes in the market, new features, marketing campaigns or even when new team members join.

Developing sales skills

In any high-performing sales team, an obsessive focus on the continual development of sales skills is an enduring source of differentiation. Alongside the Challenger Sale method, we practise 'challenger coaching' – high support and high challenge.

Sales coaching is a serious activity, and that's why I like to have fun with it. Our teams actively look forward to sessions and are energised by the whole experience. We use a variety of tools to improve sales skills in these sessions. Role play is the most fun and energetic form of sales coaching we do, and it takes various forms. For each role play, we describe a basic situation and then launch straight into a simulated conversation designed to assess a particular sales skill. We regularly focus on:

1. Prospecting

2. Qualifying

3. Selling value

4. Handling objections

5. Closing, then on to the next steps

We regularly use group role play as an energising opener (and sometimes to close) in weekly sales meetings, and we occasionally use it in daily sales huddles. Group role play creates a pressure situation for each salesperson and gives them a stage to shine on. Feedback is offered by the team as a whole in a fun and non-judgemental way. It's a supportive discussion that provides mutual experiential learning.

We reserve one-on-one role play for sharper, more focused scenarios that address individual development needs or for newer recruits who are not yet ready for the rigours of the group environment. These individual sessions can be scored to help benchmark competence and build development plans.

Whichever form of role play we conduct, it always takes place in a safe developmental environment where it's OK to take risks and make mistakes. We'd rather mistakes be made in an artificial environment with nothing commercial at risk. This relaxes and empowers our team to be authentic and try different things to see what works best for them.

Call coaching, when sales managers listen to live client calls, is perhaps the most common form of sales coaching. During the calls, the salesperson performs their normal role while the sales manager listens intently and takes notes. At the end of each call, a detailed review is performed and the learning points are noted. As with role play, the calls can be objectively scored to inform development plans. A variant of call coaching is listening to a playback of recorded calls to gain similar learning insights. The benefits of call coaching include the opportunity to observe and assess rapport-building, presentation skills and the all-important non-verbal communication skills. By systematically applying a selection of sales skills development initiatives, you can be certain of increasing your win rate, shortening your sales cycle and optimising your overall sales productivity for the highest returns.

Qualifying

Qualifying is the step that receives the least attention, yet it can be the most significant way to improve sales outcomes. Qualifying is so important because it's the part of the process that sorts the wheat from the chaff of customer enquiries. It allows you to stop the 'tyre kickers' wasting time, which is a salesperson's most precious resource. Progressing with enquiries that are destined to go nowhere will be a thing of the past once your salespeople master the simple concept of qualifying. The problem is that too many salespeople lack any form of process or rigour when qualifying opportunities – or indeed have any real awareness of how important it is.

Qualifying helps build rapport and connection with a prospect by showing empathy with their business and their individual wants and needs. It's a legitimate way to coax the client to invest in your company with their most precious asset – their time. The deeper they become invested in you, the more likely they are to make a positive buying decision with you – this is a core psychological principle. By doing some deep qualifying in this first stage of your sales process, you're demonstrating your curiosity to understand before being understood. Most people are more comfortable talking about themselves than listening to someone else. Effective qualifying gives your prospect a stage to speak on, while affording you the chance to show you're an effective listener. It's simple, but powerful.

My businesses take the 'MEANCATS' approach to qualifying, and have embraced it for the last ten years. This has been to great effect, maximising our conversion rates and shortening our sales cycle. Using the MEANCATS approach, our salespeople ask questions about the following when they deal with initial enquiries:

- **Money** – these targeted questions are designed to uncover the prospect's actual budget and how it's released, so you can decide on your price strategy for the opportunity.

    - 'What stage in the budgeting process are you at?'

    - 'What are the budgeting steps?'

    - 'What budget is allocated to the project?'

- **Emotion** – to find out what's important to the client in arriving at their decision so you can position your offering accordingly. This is usually informed by their wants and needs, but may also indicate which aspect of the price-quality-time proposition you should focus on.

    - 'What are the top three aspects of what you're looking for, in order of importance?'

- **Authority** – asking about this tells you who the decision makers are on a project so you're as certain as you can be that you're speaking to the organ grinder and not the monkey. Most inexperienced salespeople fail miserably at this step; it never crosses their mind that there may be multiple stakeholders in a decision who need to be influenced. Often in big ticket sales, a C-level executive has ultimate sign-off on the project and then delegates front-line staff to procure multiple offers.

  - 'What's the decision-making process for this procurement, and which people are involved at what stage?'

- **Need** – unless you identify your client's categoric need for your product or service, you may be whistling in the wind. I've seen salespeople waste hundreds of hours on opportunities that were mere 'fishing trips' on the part of the client. In some cases, the enquiries can be from competitors disguised as prospects, seeking to gain some competitive intelligence. Watch out for personal email addresses or random telephone calls where there's an 'urgent' need for lots of 'info' on a 'major' opportunity.

  - 'What's driven you to get in contact with us today?'

  - Then ask explorative questions depending on the answer you receive.

- **Competition** – know who you're competing against to help you position your offering. No doubt you'll have different strengths and weaknesses compared with different competitors. They'll sell against you in a certain way, and vice versa. There's a chance that you're being asked for a proposal simply to provide a benchmark against their preferred option to make up a quota of three completive offers before a decision can be made. To help reveal the competitive landscape, ask:

    - 'Who else is bidding for this work?'

    - 'What, if any, existing supply relationship do you have with them?'

- **Advantage** – understand your strengths and weaknesses relative to the buyer's wants and needs. If you can get clarity on how you stack up against your competition, you can tweak your proposition by massaging your price or by enhancing the value you deliver. You can also adjust your sales tactics to set the buyer's agenda based on your strengths and the competitors' weaknesses.

    - 'What advantages do you see with what we offer relative to the competitors, and vice versa?'

- **Timescale** – knowing the urgency involved ensures you prioritise those in your team who will deliver your monthly sales quota. It makes you as efficient as possible and allows you to decide what sales 'touches' each opportunity needs. If it's an urgent decision of significant scale, you know you probably need to get in front of the client quickly to influence the decision personally.

- 'When do you need delivery by?'

- **Scope** – asking about this gives you clarity on the extent of the opportunity; in the short term and the long term. The bigger the opportunity, the more energy and rigour you need to put into winning it. Clients don't always reveal the overall scope; occasionally, I have seen an enquiry come in about a low quantity, only to lose it and discover that it was a pilot project with significantly greater future potential.

  - 'What's the overall scope of this opportunity in the short and medium term?'

  - 'Who else in your organisation has a need?'

In our sales offices, the word MEANCATS is emblazoned on the wall as a constant reminder to consistently nail this critical foundational step to sales success.

Sales tools

Be mindful of the old adage 'a bad workman always blames his tools', since underperforming salespeople tend to look outside themselves to explain their poor sales performance. Providing them with a set of killer sales tools removes this excuse while building their confidence. Buyers can sense any hesitance from a salesperson, so anything that builds confidence is vital for better sales performance. The sales tools you develop and use will depend on what you're selling, but they may include the following:

- Product samples

- Interactive presentations

- Videos

- Brochures and leaflets

- Buyer's guides

- Competitor comparisons

- Industry guides

- Savings calculator

- Risk assessment

- Loan kit

- Demonstration kit

Major bids

Large contracts can make or break a sales quota. They're the 'manna from heaven' for any sales leader – win one, and stellar bonus payments are almost guaranteed. Winning one when you're in a sea of sharks all sensing a feeding frenzy is a different prospect altogether.

Strong competition shouldn't dissuade you, as long as your value proposition is strong. The secret with major bids lies in knowing when and if to bid, because they take so much effort; anything less than committing 100% to win them would be commercial folly. That's why using a specific process to assess each major bid opportunity will serve you well. Our major bid assessment process has six distinct steps:

1. **The pre-qualification stage,** during which we assess our reasons to bid or not, before we reach a 'go' or 'no-go' decision. This stage involves assessing our ability to win the bid, the financial value of the proposition and its strategic value to us as an organisation. We balance this against reasons not to bid, which include proposal risks and opportunity costs. We look at the balance of these to reach a 'bid' or 'no bid' decision.

2. **Selecting the team to put the bid together.** For large tenders, this means reaching across various departments to serve the varied roles required.

3. **Diving deep into the MEANCATS model,** which may uncover a strong reason *not* to bid. It's important not to ignore this.

4. **Delivering a truly remarkable bid document,** which has:

   - A brilliant executive summary.

   - Evidence that the proposed solution will meet or exceed the bid requirements.

   - Positioning statements that narrate points of differentiation, explaining why the bid deserves to be successful.

5. **Creating an 'influence' checklist,** which defines the clients' stakeholders who we need to engage with to improve our chances of success. Take care at this stage not to fall foul of bid guidelines.

6. **Preparing and rehearsing a powerful pitch.**

Whatever the outcome of a bid, there's great value in conducting a formal review, including asking for feedback from the client, to inform improvements for future bids.

I've led numerous major bids and I've enjoyed a significant success rate. Twenty years ago, I 'downed tools' to devote four weeks to compiling a bid for the Ministry of Defence, which resulted in a contract worth twice the company's annual turnover. Later, I led two successful bids to the European Union for remotely piloted helicopter services, resulting in contract awards to the value of €77 million. Whatever major bids you become involved with, ensure you make the right decision on whether to bid. For the ones you go for, throw everything at them!

You can download your personal version of our major bid template by visiting http://paulluen.com/documents

Negotiation

In life you don't get what you deserve, you get what you negotiate. Mastering this skill will put you at an advantage in life and in business. The best investment in CPD I ever made was in a two-day negotiating course twenty years ago, from which I've retained the knowledge and apply it almost weekly. I carry laminates the size of a credit card with me to remind me of the basic principles:

- **Be thoroughly prepared** – have a clear plan about how you'll conduct the negotiation – fail to plan, plan to fail.

- **Aim high to get more** – remember you can come down from an opening position, but it's almost impossible to go up.

- **Leave room in your offers to negotiate** – the other side expects it, and you'll come across as obstinate if you have nothing to give.

- **Know your tradables** – what things are of high value to the other side but low cost to you, and vice versa?

- **Don't trust your assumptions** – any assumption you have about the flexibility in the other side's position can be a self-limiting belief, leaving 'money on the table'.

- **Know your relative strengths and weaknesses** – if you don't, you may get hijacked during the negotiation.

- **Avoid quick deals** – there's value in getting the other side to really work for a deal, and if you lead it correctly you may well benefit from their concessions due to 'deal fatigue'.

You can use the following tactics and phrases at various stages of a negotiation to achieve the best possible outcomes:

- A 'flinch', where you show disbelief, is a creative tactic that works on an emotional level to put the other side on the defensive, as if what they're asking is unrealistic.

- 'Take it or leave it' works when you've gone as far as you can and you just need to get closure or pursue other options.

- 'You need to do better than that' works by implying that their current position is not acceptable or within your acceptable range.

- A 'nibble' occurs at the end of the process, where the other side thinks you've made a deal and then you ask for something extra. If it's small enough, you'll generally get it!

In all negotiations you're involved with, you'll have to be prepared to concede some ground from your opening position so you can reach a deal. When offering concessions, I apply these principles to get the best deal outcomes:

- Be stingy with concessions, and never instigate them.

- Watch the rate concessions are offered at – control the pace and don't jump in too quickly.

- If you give a concession, make it conditional on something from the other side – for example, better payment terms in return for a price reduction.

- As the deadline for a negotiation looms, don't get panicked into granting concessions to get the deal done – let the other side do that.

- Never 'split the difference', even if it seems to be a fair thing to do. When the other side suggests it, you know you can get a better deal.

Sales channels

You'll almost certainly have your own directly employed team of salespeople as your business scales, but you can increase the reach and leverage of your products and services by creating partnerships and joint ventures (JVs). A JV may be a relationship with an enterprise, an organisation, a department or even an individual who has access to a market that you have less access to. They may also have intimate access, with lower friction, to an audience that you want to target.

Creating a JV involves surrendering part of the asset value to your partner, but it's a win-win arrangement because it gives you a beneficial reach to a wider audience. Examples include appointing:

- Distributors

- Agents

- Affiliates

- Referral schemes

When Google Earth entered into a JV with NASA, a terrestrial entity with a near-global reach (Google) was able to harness the tools of an agency with access to outer space (NASA) using resources that only it could provide. It made commercial sense to both partners. As Eric Schmidt, Google's then chairman and chief executive said at the time, 'Google and NASA share a common desire, to bring a universe of information to people around the world.'[14] This is a great example of how each partner's assets complement the other, giving phenomenal leverage to both.

Whichever type of JV you pursue, its huge power is not to be underestimated. I've come across many business leaders who are reticent to engage JV partners. They fear that by working with another party, they'll be surrendering part of their profit margin. When it's done properly, a JV allows a business to unlock otherwise unattainable audiences while still allowing it to leverage and monetise its assets. It's a strategy that has certainly worked well for my businesses. Appointing local agents, with local knowledge of the market and cultural sensitivities, has opened up markets in the Far East and generated eight figure revenues. To achieve that level of penetration by our efforts alone would have been impossible. By working with JV partners, especially overseas, we significantly added to our asset bank over time and accessed a wider audience.

For any business, the underlying principle remains the same – build, borrow, buy and 'tempt' (within the rules for healthy competition) the audiences who are yet to find you. Working in a JV reduces the friction that would otherwise be generated in order for your product or service to land in front of your target

---

14   J Dino, 'NASA Takes Google On a Journey Into Space', NASA.gov, September 2005, www.nasa.gov/vision/earth/technologies/google. html

prospects. Sometimes you'll still need to do a certain amount of pivoting, or make a slight adjustment, to appeal to different audiences, but that's all part of the concept of getting the most value out of any asset across as many different audiences as possible.

KPIs

We systematically review our KPIs to help our decision making in the sales function. There are so many KPIs that you can measure and manage, and which you choose will depend on what you see as driving the right behaviours in the sales team. Remember, what is measured and managed gets done:

- Calls

- Meetings

- Proposals

- Coaching hours

- Pipeline value

- Sales qualified leads

- Lead-to-opportunity conversion rate

- Opportunity-to-won conversion rate

- Gross margin

- Sales (£)

- Number of active customers

- Amount spent per customer

We share the minimum standards of performance for each KPI. This results in competitive, hungry, driven salespeople who relish the opportunity of being top dog and equally hate bringing up the rear.

Checklist: Sales

- How aligned are your sales and marketing efforts?

- What's your sales method?

- How do you rate the core attributes of your sales team?

- How effective is your bonus scheme?

- How effective is your sales plan?

- How much time do you spend honing sales skills?

- Is qualifying a problem in your sales team?

- What sales tools do your sales team need to improve conversion?

- How good are you at winning major bids?

- What sales channels do you need to acquire and grow?

- Are you tracking the right KPIs to reveal actionable insights?

You can download your personal version of this checklist by visiting http://paulluen.com/documents

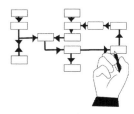

9
Systems And Processes

In the early years of any business, most of us are flying solo, sometimes with a small starter team around us. It's a close-knit affair, and we all have a good idea of what each of us is supposed to be taking care of. To some extent, we make it up as we go along. As the business slowly begins to expand and more people join, inconsistencies begin to appear; it's no longer easy to assume we know exactly what everyone else is doing. Still, the business manages to stumble along, and the jobs in hand get done (or so we think). The more it grows, the more chaos sets in. People aren't listening to each other, the same task is being handled by different people in different ways, it's difficult to track who's doing what – or why – and the whole thing is more like herding cats than running an organised business. I've seen several businesses struggling to cope with an endless circus they've unwittingly created. If we don't do anything about it, the business plateaus and falls into decline. This is why having systems, processes and rhythm is so important for sustainability and survival, not only from an operational point of view but also to reassure your clients. They'll be looking for a smoothly run, highly organised business that deserves their custom.

ISO 9001 is an international standard for quality management that's designed to build in quality and help organisations to constantly improve their product and service delivery. To meet the standard, companies have to state exactly how they carry out their business. Most decent-sized businesses become certified, but in my experience, many emerging SMEs fear this commitment or are reticent to apply. This is because they currently employ immature processing systems, which are prone to creating inconsistent rhythms in the business. Often, they don't see the value of formalising and systemising their whole operation within the ISO 9001 framework. I can't stress how important it is for all businesses, even start-ups, to plan for introducing their own quality-management systems.

I am a passionate exponent of IS0 9001 because my businesses flourished once the quality certification had been achieved. As well as focusing your attention on how you will run the business, it's a powerful indicator to your potential clients that your business has its house in order. Without it, it's highly unlikely that the business will qualify for bigger tenders, such as with government agencies or public limited companies (PLCs). The certification tells the big players that yours is a serious business that is dependable, with a consistent, reproduceable, reliable output. If your business lacks any of these, it will be viewed not only as a bit-part player but also as operating in a state of chaos, which is far from ideal.

The immediate benefits of committing to systems, process and rhythm is that you define how the business will move forward. It creates the 'business bible'; instantly, it allows you to create the framework for training new employees in a consistent way that is aligned to your values. It defines the blueprint for day-to-day operations and the back-up documents you need, while providing a platform for continual improvement. For any business looking to scale, having systems, processes and rhythms defined and in place makes it possible to repeatedly develop them, and stay agile, as the business changes. They are critical for growth and succession. As I've explained, it's the people who make the business – and in that respect, ISO 9001 requires the business to put people first.

A simple first step to introducing a quality-management system is to find a template, examine it and then adapt and configure it for your business. If this section has prompted you to take a closer look at the ISO 9001 certification process, visit the British Assessment

Bureau website (www.british-assessment.co.uk) and navigate to the 'ISO 9001 Quality Management' page.

Software systems and automation

The business world is awash with software and apps that enable business to communicate and collaborate while automating business processes and reporting. It's beyond the scope of this book to make any personal recommendations, but I encourage you to explore all the opportunities available to you. Across my businesses I've deployed cloud-based tools, such as Microsoft Office 365, Microsoft Dynamics NAV, Salesforce, Pardot and Sage, to great effect. Looking back, I could also tell you some horror stories about failed integrations that cost us tens of thousands of pounds and lots of pain!

All enterprises should automate as many processes as they can, so invest in the appropriate software at the earliest opportunity. From marketing to accounting, the sooner you research which systems can integrate and talk to each other, the better. There is plenty of 'freemium' software available to start-ups, which have low entry costs and only scale as the business does. My basic rule is to keep all processes lean, with the fewest possible steps, and then train the hell out of my people to follow each process consistently – either manually or with software automation.

Rhythms and rituals

When I wake up, I don't have to think about the first thing I do, which is to drink water: I just do it. Nor do I have to think about getting out of the bed, making myself a coffee, having some breakfast and then taking exercise. I just do it. The whole process is automatic. If I have to think about one thing, I can't think about another at the same time, but my innate rhythm relieves me of the burden of sweating the small stuff. That frees up my mind to think about the more important things. The same principle applies to business. As a leader, a manager, an entrepreneur, an intrapreneur or a solopreneur, your job, as much as possible, is to work *on* your enterprise and not *in* it. If you're working too much *in* it then you're doing work that's way below your pay grade and inadvertently diminishing your team. Remember, that's what I was doing when I began my business.

Back when I hadn't given any thought to putting systems and processes in place, I'd stumble into the day. There'd be times where I'd forget my phone or my laptop, or I would get to work and find that a critical device wasn't charged up. My daily rhythm was f*cked, because there was no structure to it. Today, I couldn't be more different: before I leave the office, whatever papers I need to look at the next morning I place ready on my desk. The moment I get home, I put all my devices on charge and my rucksack in a certain place. After that, I'm free to enjoy my evening, which involves winding down and spending time with family. I've evolved this rhythm by working on myself and by working with some great people, who have shown me by their example that it works to have a rhythm that doesn't use up any thinking capacity. It frees me from worrying or thinking about all the irrelevancies, so that I can attend to the really important matters that improve the outcomes of the business.

Why is rhythm so important for you as a leader? It's simple: unless you demonstrate a 'systems thinking' approach to your team, you'll be in a state of chaos and your team will subconsciously follow that lead. That realisation marked a big shift in my mindset. I'd always thought of myself as a naturally creative thinker, the 'big ideas' person who didn't need any sort of structure. I was more inclined to throw loads of ideas onto the table, because I was always researching the latest thing. Unconsciously 'addicted to chaos', I never managed to see those ideas through, so many of them never amounted to much or delivered real value.

Chaos and stress are the inevitable outcomes of having no systems, processes or rhythm in place. I'm frequently shocked at the number of companies I observe, some of which are bigger and more established than my own, that lack systems and process. I'm convinced that rigorously implementing ISO 9001 certified systems and processes was a significant factor in being able to sell one of my businesses to a £1billion market cap PLC for an eight-figure sum. One of the key reasons that they decided to acquire and invest in us was because of the maturity of our systems and processes, which belied the fact that we were a £10million turnover SME. For our investor partner, our certification mitigated any risk. This is a major consideration if you intend to scale and grow your business through investment. If how this happens is solely down to you as a business owner, without any evidence of systems and processes, that's a danger sign.

Leadership meeting rhythms

The most important 'rhythm' that serves me and my businesses is the culture of meetings held with leadership teams and other managers. This culture and its rhythms have been refined over many years to support the definition and execution of our business strategy while upholding our values.

Daily check-in

Every day we hold a fifteen-minute meeting at precisely 10am. The time of the meeting allows people to attend to their early morning agendas, reflect on the opportunities and challenges of the day ahead, and think about the support they need from their peers. The topics we cover typically include:

- Critical numbers* – specific successes and actions

- Dashboard exceptions review – actionable insight only, what is being done to address them or celebrate them

- Challenges or bottlenecks that need action

- Important information

- Any other business

* All my businesses obsess over two critical numbers on a daily basis – the numbers which have most relevance to driving growth and around which I stimulate daily conversations: number of active customers and £/customer. One number should be the balance of the other.

Weekly tactical

We set this for one hour each Tuesday at 2pm. The agenda is slightly longer than for the daily check-in:

- Any outstanding actions from last meeting – who, what, when

- 60s manager dept update – news, events, key priorities for week ahead

- Management information dashboard exceptions review

- Our people and culture – exceptions and opportunities

- Customer success improvement opportunities and actions
- Quarterly priorities execution progress review and recovery actions

Any other business: monthly review

At these meetings we delve into the leadership team's monthly report pack and review the overall financial performance of the business for the previous month.

- Any outstanding actions from last meeting – who, what, when
- Board pack review – questions to leaders
- Profit and cash improvement opportunities
- Productivity improvement opportunities
- Sustainability improvement opportunities
- Monthly topic 'deep dive'
- QHSE and internal audits
- Innovation opportunities
- Any other business

Quarterly strategic review

Each quarter, we review the last three months and plan the strategy for the three months to come. This is all supplemented by the annual planning process.

☑ **Agenda**

☐ 9.00 YTD & Q4 Financial Forecast Review – consider any recovery actions for any observed Q4 or YTD exceptions to MSOP

☐ 9.15 Critical numbers – consider any recovery actions for any observed Q4 or YTD exceptions to MSOP

☐ 9.30 New challenges and opportunities – Parking Lot Review

☐ 10.00 Bottlenecks/stuck points

☐ 10.15 Pareto analysis 80/20 – what 20% of activity in each area delivers 80% of the results

☐ 10.30 Customer feedback/trends/complaints to address

☐ 11.00 24 Assets – what can we develop/curate in Q4?

☐ 11.30 People, attitudes & behaviours we need to work on

☐ 12.00 Competences/resources we need to develop/acquire – KRAs, IGTs next steps/sustainability

☐ 12.15 How to impart more freedom and ownership around execution of objectives

☐ 12.30 LUNCH

☐ 13.00 Draft AP cards

☐ 14.30 Assign owners

☐ 14.45 Are proposed Q priorities the REAL priorities – what have we missed?

☐ 15.00 Review & SMART stress test each QP

☐ 16.00 Overall review – is it achievable?

Sample agenda: quarterly strategic review

Everything we do in these meetings is consistently structured, and everybody knows what's on their calendar for the coming twelve months. This gives us control and security and sets the business up for success. All other meetings are framed around delivering 'desired outcomes' and are held only if the outcome has been agreed. I don't accept a meeting request unless it's clear what the required outcomes are. If anyone suggests you have a casual meeting over coffee or lunch without defining an agenda, avoid wasting your time.

Parkinson's law

Parkinson's law is the adage that work expands so as to fill the time available for its completion. For example, if you give yourself two hours to complete a task, you'll fill that time. If instead you allocate a shorter amount of time to the task, you are much more productive and the quality of your output is similar. Set short deadlines for all deliverables, and then you'll develop a much more productive enterprise.

The 'parking lot'

I constantly have loads of ideas, as I bet you do too. I used to cause chaos by asking people to act on these ideas immediately, which they duly did. Usually, this would be at the expense of something else: often, the execution of their priority tasks, which were key in driving business results. Guess what? We had weak execution and were often chopping and changing, with a lack of clarity on which matters were really the most important.

Today we're much stronger at resisting the 'shiny new objects' and have a mature process that places all new ideas in a 'parking lot' until they can be reviewed at the quarterly meetings. We still retain the option to go with something new if it's too good an opportunity to ignore after a stress test, but these are few and far between. As a result, we now execute ideas with a high level of success and everyone feels like they're winning more often, which is crucial to organisational culture.

Avoiding interruptions and distractions

To avoid interruptions and distractions, the policy across my business is that no personal phones are visible in the workplace and all notifications are turned off. Our blanket policy is also for all email notifications to be turned off. This helps people to focus and control their agenda, rather than being slaves to the 'ping' of the inbox. This isn't a draconian measure that infringes people's liberties; it's about creating a workplace ethos that keeps distractions to the minimum so we can focus on getting things done.

According to research by Microsoft, responding to a single email can take twenty-five minutes.[15] The *Irish Times* reported a cluster of research results that showed the average person picks up their phone

---

15 S T Iqbal and E Horvitz, *Disruption and Recovery of Computing Tasks: Field study, analysis, and directions* (Microsoft, 2007)

fifty-five times a day,[16] while in the USA that figure is reportedly higher at eighty times a day.[17]

Here's the science:

- **It saps our time.** Every time you get interrupted – when your phone buzzes with a new message or your Gmail tab compels you to check the inbox – you lose twenty minutes. According to a University of California-Irvine study, that's how long it takes to reacquaint yourself with the details of what you were doing before.[18]

- **It makes us dumber.** A psychiatrist at King's College London University found that fussing with your email leads to a functional drop of ten IQ points – more than you would lose if you smoked marijuana![19]

- **It slows us down.** Research shows that switching between tasks takes up to 40% longer than doing one task at a time.[20]

---

16 C Pope, 'Average Irish Smartphone User Picks up 55 Times a Day', *Irish News*, 2018, www.irishtimes.com/news/consumer/average-irish-smartphone-user-picks-up-55-times-a-day-survey-1.3703348

17 SWNS, 'Americans Check their Phones 80 Times a Day', *New York Post*, 2017, https://nypost.com/2017/11/08/americans-check-their-phones-80-times-a-day-study

18 G Mark, V M Gonzalez and J Harris, 'No task left behind? Examining the nature of fragmented work', CHI 2005, 321–330, www.ics.uci.edu/~gmark/CHI2005.pdf

19 'Emails "hurt IQ more than pot"', *CNN International*, 2005, http://edition.cnn.com/2005/WORLD/europe/04/22/text.iq

20 'Multitasking: Switching costs', American Psychological Association, March 2006, www.apa.org/research/action/multitask

Checklist: systems and processes

- How much chaos exists in your organisation because it lacks systems and processes?

- Where does ISO 9001 sit on your priorities?

- What software and automation could revolutionise your business productivity and customer experience?

- How do you rate your internal rhythms and rituals?

- What's missing from your leadership team meetings?

- Where can you gainfully apply Parkinson's law?

- Do you have tendencies to pursue 'shiny new objects' instead of your strategic priorities?

- How addicted to distraction is your team?

- How much do you tolerate interruptions?

- What's a lack of focus on deep work costing you or your organisation?

You can download your personal version of this checklist by visiting http://paulluen.com/documents

10
Inspiring Leadership

Recruiting great people is one thing, retaining them in an inspiring high-performance culture is another. If you've followed a rigorous recruitment process, you're likely to have attracted the talent that's absolutely right for your business. You've sold the dream to them by describing all the brilliant qualities of your business. Now it's up to you to deliver on those promises through your inspirational leadership.

For me, leadership is about placing people at the heart of everything we do. No one works for the firm; everybody works for themselves. It's about influence rather than authority, an outdated leadership model. It's about building a company that can tick along without a 'leader', while relentlessly stimulating progress towards results with great humility and professional will.

Your job is to create a climate where the truth is heard while retaining the unwavering faith that your business will survive and thrive, no matter what is thrown at you. You'll need to devote your time to organisational design where 'good enough' is never good enough, expecting more and better every year, creating internal competition and discomfort. Risk management is another key facet of leadership: you'll need to identify and control 'death risks', which could kill the business, and eliminate 'asymmetrical risks', where the downside is bigger than the upside.

I am forever looking to unite everybody around a common vision, mission and set of values, doing everything I can to cheerlead the whole organisation around these principles. As a leader, it's my responsibility to live and breathe my vision, mission and values and to ensure that I communicate these regularly, little and often, with absolute transparency. It's my job to behave in complete alignment with my values to pursue that vision while living the mission of the business.

The CEO

The convention is that CEO is an abbreviation for chief executive officer. Rather unconventionally, I like to think that it stands for three areas of responsibility:

1. Chief education officer

2. Chief energy officer

3. Chief entertainment officer

Here's how I approach each of those aspects:

Educate

For anybody joining my business culture, it's quite a big step up to meet the expectation that they'll spend at least forty hours a year on their own CPD. Most embrace it wholeheartedly and spend more than 100 hours a year on their learning. I consider that a huge personal success, as I'm passionate about creating a nurturing workplace environment that enables freedom of thought, development and expression. In my opinion, anchoring learning lies at the heart of everything in any business, and the results are transformative for all concerned. I'm forever seeking opportunities to transfer knowledge and skill and to impart wisdom in applying that knowledge and skill. For me, it's about continually cultivating a living and breathing learning organisation.

Energise

Energy in a business is contagious and when it's in abundance, it spreads with remarkable speed. The shadow I cast as a leader is critical, and the energy I radiate comes in various forms. I love catching people doing the right thing and celebrating success in the moment with great gusto. Then there's the more subtle type of energy, the non-verbal communication, which I'm careful with. The impact of gestures and facial expressions can be huge. When I'm addressing an audience, the pitch and pace of my narrative needs careful attention and the use of gentle pauses all serve to create the right energy and attention in a room.

Entertain

The serious foundations of the business must be built on the fact that the work environment needs to be fun. Enjoyment is a foundational value in my businesses, and it's one that we all hold ourselves accountable to. We want a sense of levity, where people are free to be their authentic selves and to speak and act just as they would with family and friends. When I walk the four corners of my businesses, I'm actively looking to have fun encounters with the team, telling stories and exchanging jokes. At company social events I'm happy to be the one dressing up, first on the karaoke or making an ass out of myself. I'm not suggesting our businesses should be run like holiday camps or booze cruises, as that would certainly be counterproductive, but people spend so much of their waking lives at work that they deserve to be entertained. Remember that what one person might deem 'fun' might be another person's worst nightmare, though. You can't force fun and it can't be imposed on anyone, so don't.

Part of our approach is to empower each department to create their own fun, using an agreed 'fun budget'. It's up to the team leaders and their colleagues to decide how they spend that, be it going to the dogs or bowling, booking a nice restaurant for lunch, or taking a trip to the theatre. They can also use it to bring a professional into the office, such as a masseur, chiropractor, podiatrist or nail technician. It's about creating those moments when people – yes, those vibrant human beings with senses of humour and unlimited curiosity – can try new things and engage with each other as the social animals they are. The only stipulation is that however each department decides to spend the fun budget, it has to drive team engagement. If a spend is fun, gets everybody talking and keeps the team bonds strong and healthy, they can do as they please.

General leadership environment

If you create a pleasant working environment, people's energy levels will increase. You can do this with simple touches, such as displaying inspirational quotes and images on the walls, or creating open spaces for easy socialising with free drinks and snacks available. In my businesses we work in open-plan spaces, with no glass walls to create hierarchies. We have greenery, vending machines, and cooking facilities with 'break-out' areas. There's table football and darts for those cheeky bets and competitions. Employees can reserve meeting rooms with conventional or standing desks depending on the energy they want to create for a task or meeting. We have the radio or Spotify playing in the background – at the right volume, it's proven to increase engagement and productivity. On the walls are charts and our 'KPI dashboard' – visual metrics to show us how we're doing. A bell gets rung to celebrate sales orders. I'm constantly looking to develop the environment in response to feedback and put employee experience at the heart of our facilities.

Transparency

A survey carried out in 2014 for the American Psychological Association showed that nearly 25% of employees didn't trust their employer.[21] If the people I work with felt the same way about me, I would be gutted. Transparency builds relationships, and innovation tops the Forbes List for fostering employee

---

21 'Employee Distrust is Pervasive in U.S. Workforce', American Psychological Association, 2014, www.apa.org/news/press/releases/2014/04/employee-distrust

happiness and boosting innovation.[22] I couldn't agree more, and that's borne out by the fact that in my businesses we prefer people to feel relaxed while they're at work.

Some years ago, I came to the realisation that trust and transparency are critical in a business. How a business communicates internally is key to achieving that. The infamous 'grapevine' is often nothing better than gossip and rumour; it's an untrustworthy and potentially damaging medium for internal communication. It's not a healthy way for people to learn about what's going on, or what the future plans are. Today, we follow formal and transparent comms protocols. At the end of every week, during our leadership team meeting, we discuss what we need to communicate to the entire workforce. That can include new product updates, development plans, plans for hiring new talent, feedback from an employee leaving the business, and financial news. Each quarter, we share with absolute transparency the full commercial performance of the business. That includes sales revenue, profit and loss numbers and strategic planning. On that level, we keep the whole company in the loop through our formal channels.

Alongside this, we communicate with managers and teams on a more informal daily basis to share 'break-

---

22 W Craig, '10 Things Transparency Can Do for Your Company', *Forbes*, 2018, www.forbes.com/sites/williamcraig/2018/10/16/10-things-transparency-can-do-for-your-company/#630e760725d0

ing news' when something significant happens that might affect them soon or directly, be it positive or negative. The last thing we want is for a manager to find out important information from one of their team: that's not only demoralising but also irritating.

Situational leadership

Situational leadership helps diagnose the appropriate levels of support and direction that individual employees need to fulfil certain tasks in their roles. Embracing this concept, which was developed and studied by Kenneth Blanchard and Paul Hersey (situational.com), was a breakthrough for me. Blanchard and Hersey suggest that no single leadership 'one size fits all' style is best practice; instead, leadership styles need to be adapted to suit the task in hand. No two situations or individuals will be exactly the same, so the most effective leaders are the ones who can adapt their style to a specific situation while taking a 360-degree view. This includes looking at the task itself, the people (or person) who is responsible for the task, and any other factors that might contribute towards achieving a positive outcome.

For example, a new employee in an unfamiliar role will not have all the knowledge they need, but they will probably have a high level of commitment. In this scenario, a low-direction and supportive leadership style would be appropriate. At the other extreme, an employee with extensive experience who also performs well (high competence and high commitment) is likely to be a self-reliant achiever who needs little support and who can be challenged to stretch themselves even further with high direction in a delegating style. Understanding the principles of situational leadership and applying them in a way that meets the employee's need for support and direction can be instrumental in a high-performance culture.

It's important to get this right: if a leader creates a highly supportive environment that lacks challenge, it can lead to gross underperformance because it's too cosy and soft. The antithesis is a highly challenging environment that lacks support, which leads to low performance because it creates stress. I spend a lot of time thinking about how I can support teams, and where I can offer a high degree of challenge when I spot a growth opportunity for an individual. That's when the magic happens. A high-performance culture develops in an environment where all leaders are highly supportive *and* highly challenging, and when the levels of support and challenge are adjusted on the basis of individuals, tasks and scenarios.

Succession planning

A key aspect of a leader's role is to grow future leaders. At some point, we all need cover, either because of holidays or because we fall ill. Without any succession policy or plans in place, if the worst were to happen to a business leader, that business would soon begin to suffer the negative consequences.

When I look back to my early career, I didn't have a clue about this area. Today I'm convinced I'd be much further forward if I'd have thought sooner about recruiting people who could step into my shoes. It pays to stay ahead of the game, so we all need to be growing future leaders to take on aspects of our role when we move on. That means taking opportunities for people to extend their comfort zone as part of their long-term development plan. Aim to transfer as much knowledge and skill as quickly as possible to create a path for succession, while elevating your own leadership trajectory.

I was able to sell a business in 2018 because I did have a succession plan in place, which meant that the value of the business wasn't intrinsically linked to me. Had that not been the case, the value of the business would have been much lower because the buyer would have placed too much value in me as an individual, making it a riskier decision for them to buy. The value needs to be in the business, not the individual. It all goes back to the idea that when you allow yourself the time and space to hand over control to key employees, you're more free to work *on* the business, and not *in* the business (and, by default, not to *be* the business at the same time).

360-degree surveys

Every six months I encourage my teams to complete an anonymous survey that allows them to rate me as a leader. I want them to offer me specific feedback on what I need to stop doing, what I need to start doing, what I need to do more of, and what I need to do less of. It's the only way I can truly feel the pulse of my performance as a leader. These surveys are a complete surrender of ego, and if you've never done one before they're a total leap of faith.

Perception is reality and so, whether I agree with the feedback or not, it gives me some guidance on what's working (or not) and where I may need to change. It's always a revealing exercise and because I openly share the results, it builds trust. The feedback I've received through 360-degree surveys has been key to developing my emotional intelligence, revealing my blind spots and highlighting my constraining behaviours to enable real change for good.

I'm happy to admit to my mistakes, and it's immensely powerful to do so publicly. 'Sorry' is such an empowering word in leadership. Linked to that is the ability to be flexible – it's OK to make a U-turn when you need to. In life we make U-turns all the time; everybody gets it wrong from time to time. I once read that it's OK to err, but if the rubber on the pencil expires before the pencil does then you've got the ratio wrong.

Leadership isn't about having a role or title. It's about serving the needs of your tribe: understanding what their wants and needs are, then making every reasonable effort to meet them. Do that, and the reciprocity principle kicks in to deliver epic performance. A 360-degree survey or other way of gaining honest feedback is one way you can make sure you're achieving this.

My key leadership attributes

- Only do what only you can do.

- Communicate, communicate, communicate – with passion and integrity.

- Obsess about self-development and personal responsibility.

- Develop your delegation ability and invest in coaching competence (Liz Wiseman's excellent *Multipliers: How the best leaders make everyone smarter*[23] is one of the best books I've read on this).

- Give people just too much to do, then let them get on with it.

- Prioritise listening over talking – ask difficult questions and then 'What else?'

---

23 L Wiseman, *Multipliers: How the best leaders make everyone smarter* (Harper Business, 2015)

- Get comfortable with uncomfortable conversations and conflict.

- Stop solving people's problems and inadvertently accepting back-delegation.

- Be less accessible – value your time so people who follow you value theirs.

Checklist: Inspiring leadership

- How united is your team around your vision, mission and values?

- Are you living, breathing and cheerleading your vision, mission and values?

- How well are you energising your team?

- Where does education sit in your leadership behaviours?

- How much do you entertain your team to create productive efficacy?

- How much fun is there in your workplace?

- Is yours an environment designed for people to excel in?

- How can you improve the transparency of your communications?

- How can you build more trust within your teams?

- How flexible is your leadership style?

- What do you really know about how your team perceive and rate you? Are you scared of finding out?

- What incentivises your people in the long term?

You can download your personal version of this check-list by visiting http://paulluen.com/documents

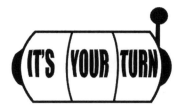

11
It's Your Turn Now

For years now, one of my goals has been to die young at a very old age. I'm the first to admit that for many of the early years of my life, I made it up as I went along. I didn't have any real clarity as to what I really wanted to do with my life or what I wanted out of it for myself, my family and my business. Looking back, I certainly wasn't set up for a long, happy, healthy life.

The truth in the old adage 'life's too short' mustn't be ignored. That reality was something I was afraid of in the past, but I'm thankful that I woke up to it: today, I'm filled with positivity and excited by possibility everywhere I turn. I embrace life and all its delights and challenges every day because, as we all know, we only get one stab at it. Why wouldn't any of us want to make it the longest, most fulfilling life we possibly can? That realisation occurred to me as I made more space in my life for self-reflection and worked with some incredible, inspirational coaches. The desire to live a long, healthy life became even stronger when I watched Nir Barzilai's inspiring TED talk about dying young at a very old age.[24] My mission statement reflects that. Some might say it's audacious, or even crazy, but I don't care: I want to live and stay 'young' until I'm 120, and for the rest of my life I'm dedicating myself to nurturing others to be the best version of themselves that they can.

If you're wondering what place this mantra of mine has in a business book, I'll tell you: begin with the end in mind. If you set that as your course – to die young at a very old age and have a clear sense of life purpose – you can work backwards to design your life in a way that will keep you heading in the right direction. For some people their purpose might be to raise amazing children; for others it's to transform a community, or to become the epitome of sporting or business success. The list goes on.

It doesn't matter what your purpose is, as long as you have that clarity about why you are here. Knowing what your personal visions and missions are, and then deciding how they apply to each area of your life, is a great way to start really living. The 'wheel of

---

24   N Barzilai, *How to Die Young at a Very Old Age* [TED talk], 2014, www.youtube.com/watch?v=TsA4SHhUzt4

life' is a useful tool for looking at how far each aspect of your life is aligned with your vision and missions.

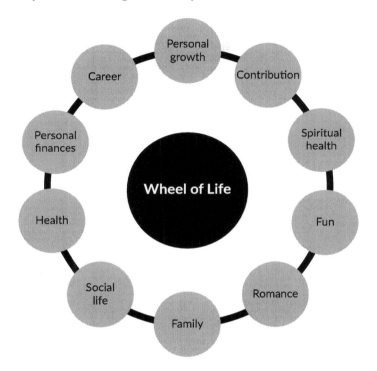

Wheel of life

As an exercise, score yourself between one and ten for each area shown in the 'wheel'. Then draw a line connecting each area to the next so you create your own wheel. If you're living your life well and in balance, the scores will be quite stable and as the wheel turns you'll have a smooth ride. If, for example, you score ten for your career and finance but five or less for health, family, friends and romance, with random scores everywhere else, it'll be much more of a rocky ride. That's the wheel of life!

You may be expecting me to tell you how this relates to business. In the short term, it doesn't, because you can still function while you're out of balance. A car can survive with a broken suspension coil for some time, but it's not sustainable. If your life is out of balance and you don't do anything to put it back in balance, it will degrade. Eventually, it'll tip over into something potentially catastrophic: anything from a major health scare to the loss of a relationship or the onset of depression. No matter what it is, it's certain to happen, but it will happen so gradually that you won't notice the signs. If you put a frog in warm water and heat that water slowly, the frog won't jump out – it'll just boil to death. That's another way of looking at the gradual creep of imbalance. If you don't do anything, it could be too late to recover.

We all find ourselves getting out of balance in certain areas of our lives at some point. Being aware of that imbalance, though, is the key to avoiding the tipping point. You can then start to work on regaining balance in your life. Over the years, I've striven to continually improve in all areas of life to achieve more balance, especially in relation to purpose and pleasure. A few years ago, I realised that my life was too heavy on purpose, without enough focus on pleasure. I was missing out on fun, romance, family and friends, and my health and wellbeing were suffering too, since my life was entirely business-centric. I had the cars, the house, the clothes and the holidays, but that was all bollocks. I'd been seduced by the fantasy that the more money and business success I achieved, the happier I would be – but in fact the opposite was true. I'd allowed the success of the business to define me, and that's where I was directing all my efforts. My wife, family, friends and health didn't really get a look-in.

If anybody had asked me what made me happy, I would have struggled to answer, because all I knew was the business side to my life. When it came to life skills, I was pretty much incompetent. It wasn't until I was on holiday in Ibiza with the lads that one of them noticed I was flat as a pancake. He turned to me and said, 'You've got mojo-nitis.' He was right. I'd lost my mojo and was a pale impression of my normal self. There I was, in one of my favourite parts of the world, with some of my favourite people, and I just didn't have anything to give. I was out of balance. It was a horrible experience, but it was an epiphany for me: I thought to myself, 'Something has got to change here.'

Be and experience who you are

I now know that I was too attached to material goals. I'm not knocking aspirations to own a dream house or a fast car, but eventually the pursuit of those goals starts to feel hollow. Before you know it, you're on the lookout for what's next. What I've since learned is that I gain a greater sense of fulfilment from living life more experientially – outdoors and offline. This can result in transformative growth or allows me to explore something that stirs my imagination, seems rich and immersive or reveals events that create a story to tell. These all involve some form of connecting with other people, and they have become my new goals. I'm now more mindful to pursue much deeper experiences through which I can learn something about myself or nurture others to become happier and more fulfilled.

The pursuit of material success can feel like a rite of passage, but if that pursuit is left unchecked and our life is out of balance, we run the risk of reaching the end of our careers, having a heart attack or seeing our relationships dwindle to nothing and wondering if it was all worth it. Keep chasing your dreams, but be more aware of what they really represent. There aren't many gravestones with an epitaph that reads, 'This guy had a Lamborghini. He drove two Ferraris and a Porsche. He lived in this really cool house. He wore designer clothes and Christian Louboutin boots.' What you will read are testimonies like 'An amazing servant to the community' or 'A kind and loving father, dearly missed by his four children and seventeen grandchildren'. There'll be nothing about how much money the person earned or what possessions they had; it'll be all about the being and the experiencing, and that's where my focus now lies.

Today, people will say that I'm more relaxed to be around and that I'm less exhausting. I'm still challenging, and in business I like to push our teams to achieve a work rate that our competitors would never reasonably expect their own teams to accomplish. That's only possible because of the culture, where everyone has complete clarity about what's expected of them, which gives them control and self-empowerment. That results in more fulfilment, engagement and happiness, and, ultimately, a higher level of business performance.

My truths

- I can deal with any situation.

- Life is not fair.

- Everything that happens comes and goes.

- Disappointments are tough, but keep them in perspective.

- Happiness can be found in many ways.

- It's the way we deal with things, not what happens, that gives us peace of mind.

- Every day is precious.

Breaking free

- If it frightens you, do it.

- Don't settle. Every time you settle, you get exactly what you settled for.

- Put yourself first.

- No matter what happens, you will handle it.

- Whatever you do, do it 100%.

- If you do what you have always done, you will get what you have always got.

- You are the only person on this planet responsible for your needs, wants and happiness.

- Ask for what you want.

- If what you are doing isn't working, try something different.

- Be clear and direct.

- Learn to say 'no'.

- Don't make excuses.

- If you are an adult, you are old enough to make your own rules.

- Let people help you.

- Be honest with yourself.

- Don't let anyone treat you badly. No one. Ever.

- Remove yourself from a bad situation instead of waiting for the situation to change.

- Never tolerate the intolerable.

- Stop blaming. Victims never succeed.

- Live with integrity. Decide what feels right to you, and then do it.

- Accept the consequences of your actions.

- Be good to yourself.

- Think 'abundance'.

- Face difficult situations and conflict head on.

- Don't do anything in secret.

- Do it now.

- Be willing to let go of what you have so you can get what you want.

- Have fun. If you aren't having fun, something is wrong.

- Give yourself room to fail. There are no mistakes, only learning experiences.

- Control is an illusion. Let go. Let life happen.

Checklist: It's your turn now

- How well are you set up to live a long and happy life?

- How balanced is your wheel of life, and what needs to change?

- Does the pursuit of material success leave you feeling hollow?

- Are you always on the lookout for 'what's next'?

- What are your personal truths?

You can download your personal version of this checklist by visiting http://paulluen.com/documents

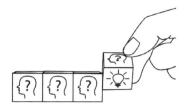

Conclusion

Now that you've taken time to reflect on the areas I've singled out in this book, you should be ready to diagnose which ones need your attention. Perhaps you've been surprised to find that you need to work on some areas of your business life or your personal life, or both. Whatever areas you decide to direct your attention to, now is the time to act if you want to make a lasting and impactful change in your life.

The question to ask yourself is: 'What would be the cost of not acting, and how would that affect my future finances and my wellbeing?' Weighing it all up will help you decide what plan you need to develop and who you'll need to engage and uplift as part of your journey. By sharing and engaging with others, you're lightening the burden on yourself and sharing some of the magic when it happens. I'm confident that when you're working your way through the process I've described, you'll realise that you're not alone, because what you've read has been tried and tested.

If, in any way, this book has inspired you, I hope you'll translate your discoveries into deliverables to change your career outcomes and positively influence the direction and outcomes of your life. What's also important is to define how you'll measure the change in those outcomes, especially if you publicly commit – which I encourage you to do – to drive accountability. Remember, the easiest person to lie to is yourself. Decide how often you'll check your progress and reflect on your improved outcomes. If you always do what you've always done, don't be surprised when you get what you've always got. If you know in your heart that there's more work to be done and more success to be won, make a cast-iron commitment to yourself that you're going to make some changes.

My aim throughout the book has been to encourage you to embrace a growth mindset and to renew, or define, your sense of purpose in your business and life, ensuring that you maintain a healthy balance in the pursuit of purpose and pleasure. Success in both areas will take you as far as possible towards living a long, rich and rewarding life and dying young at an old age. I also wanted to help you avoid many of the mistakes I've made and the pain that I've been through: sleepless nights, lost connections, burnout and a struggle to break through glass ceilings. I hope I have played a part in your achieving more quickly the success you dream of and, in doing so, becoming happier and healthier and living longer. I want you to find your true purpose and values, and align your choices with them so you can live the biggest life you can. When you feel the magic working, I'd love it if you'd 'pay it forward' and share that magic with as many people as you can.

Remember the eulogy in Chapter Three, when you were listening to the words spoken about the person who had died: what they achieved, what they meant to their friends and family, and the part they played in their community. One day, this will be your funeral. What will be said about you when you eventually expire? What actions will you take now to make sure it's a celebration of an amazing life, lived well, to a very old age? Those decisions now lie in your hands. It's time to act.

Your life is an autobiography, so write a f@cking epic.

Acknowledgements

To:

Mum and Dad – for engendering a strong work ethic and personal discipline, fundamental to everything I do;

Nikki, Luca and Ava – for brutally keeping my feet on the ground;

Steve and Mike – for being with me every step of the way on our twenty-five years of adventure;

Hayley and Susie – for the tough conversations that unlocked so much more than I expected.

Finally, I am grateful to the numerous authors and inspirational thought leaders who have helped enrich and inform my life and learning. You can discover them for yourself by downloading my recommended list at http://paulluen.com/documents.

The Author

Paul Luen is one of the most influential entrepreneurs of his generation. Since 2000 his portfolio of start-up companies has generated eight figure revenues in over one hundred countries, creating hundreds of jobs.

Paul is a natural entrepreneur – at seven years of age he was picking blackberries to sell outside the local supermarket, and as a teenager he bought blank video cassettes to sell to his classmates. Even after starting his first job, his side hustle was buying cars at auction and then selling them in *Autotrader*.

In 2000, he founded Martek Marine to improve the safety and performance of commercial ships, selling it in 2019 for eight figures, while remaining as CEO. In 2010, he established the not-for-profit Renewables Network to help businesses enter the renewable energy sector. Passionate about disruptive technology, he founded Coptrz in 2016 with a mission to revolutionise organisation using drones.

He has diversified into property establishing a multi-million-pound portfolio, and his company, Lucava (named after his kids Luca and Ava), is focused on residential development while unlocking hidden wealth for landowners.

Paul's business acumen has been recognised by numerous business awards including two Queen's Awards for Enterprise. He has a first-class honours degree in chemistry and has invested over £1 million in professional development. He has also served as a Director at Hull KR rugby league club and has a number of non-executive appointments mentoring entrepreneurs and companies to achieve their dreams.

If you'd like to arrange a free 15-minute diagnostic session with Paul, please get in touch.

✉ pl@lucava.co.uk

Printed in Great Britain
by Amazon